WARRIOR 170

ROMAN GUARDSMAN
62 BC–AD 324

ROSS COWAN   ILLUSTRATED BY SEÁN Ó'BRÓGÁIN

Series editor Marcus Cowper

ISBN: 978 1 78200 925 2
E-book ISBN: 978 1 78200 926 9
PDF ISBN: 978 1 78200 927 6

Editorial by Ilios Publishing Ltd, Oxford, UK (www.iliospublishing.com)
Index by Zoe Ross
Typeset in Myriad Pro and Sabon
Artwork by Seán Ó'Brógáin
Originated by PDQ Media, UK
Printed in China through Worldprint Ltd.

14 15 16 17 18 10 9 8 7 6 5 4 3 2 1

Osprey Publishing is supporting the Woodland Trust, the UK's leading
woodland conservation charity, by funding the dedication of trees.

www.ospreypublishing.com

ACKNOWLEDGEMENTS

The author would like to thank all those who made photographs available.
Special thanks to the Cowan family, Dr Duncan B. Campbell, Marcus
Cowper, Dan Diffendale, Dr Florian Himmler, Professor Lawrence Keppie,
Thomas McGrory, Seán Ó'Brógáin, Jasper Oorthuys, Steven D. P. Richardson,
and Dr Jean MacIntosh Turfa and the University of Pennsylvania Museum of
Archaeology and Anthropology. Quotations from ancient literary sources
have been adapted from the Loeb Classical Library.

ARTIST'S NOTE

Readers may care to note that the original paintings from which the colour
plates in this book were prepared are available for private sale. The
Publishers retain all reproduction copyright whatsoever. All enquiries
should be addressed to:

Seán Ó'Brógáin Srath an Ghallaigh, An Clochan, Leifear, Tir Chonaill, Ireland

The Publishers regret that they can enter into no correspondence upon
this matter.

CONTENTS

ROMAN GUARDSMAN, 62 BC–AD 324

INTRODUCTION

For four centuries, from the civil wars of the Late Republic to Constantine's bloody reunification of the Empire, elite units of guardsmen were at the heart of every Roman army. Whether as bodyguards or as shock troops in battle, the fighting skills of praetorians, *speculatores*, *custodes* and *singulares* determined the course of Roman history.

The reputation of Roman guardsmen, especially those belonging to the Imperial praetorian cohorts, is bad. There was a suspicion that they were lazy and battle-shy, that their role as guards in the great metropolis of Rome, with all its distractions, enervated them as soldiers and made them greedy and susceptible to corruption and treachery. But if the praetorians were so bad, why did the emperors retain them for so long?

It cannot be denied that the praetorians assassinated or abandoned a considerable number of emperors, but it will be shown that their motivations were complex and bound up with Roman notions of honour and codes of acceptable behaviour.

We will explore the fascinating history of the praetorians, and their fellow guardsmen, from their first appearance in battle at Pistoria in 62 BC, to their heroic last stand by the Milvian Bridge in AD 312, and consider the afterlife of the old guards units up to AD 324. We will follow guardsmen through recruitment and training and examine their varied duties, including sentry

A much restored relief from the Arch of Claudius (AD 51), depicting praetorian guardsmen. The heads of the figures in the foreground are restored, and the helmets of all the soldiers are the result of artistic licence, but the decorated muscle cuirass of the officer (a tribune?), the curved oval *scuta*, and the heavy *pila* may be taken as accurate depictions of praetorian equipment. The legionary-type eagle standard harks back to the Late Republic when praetorians were selected from the best legionaries. (© A. Rézette)

duty in Rome, firefighting, and pursuing bandits through the Italian countryside. We will consider the tactical organization of the guards units, and see how they were used in battle.

This book will dispel the popular image of the unworthy Roman guardsman, who will be revealed as ferociously loyal, highly trained and always ready for action.

CHRONOLOGY

62 BC	Marcus Petreius' praetorian cohort breaks Sullan veterans at Pistoria.
49 BC	Praetorian cohort of *caetrati* in Marcus Petreius' army in Spain.
44 BC	Caesar dismisses Spanish bodyguards; Marc Antony and Octavian form guard units from Caesar's veterans.
43 BC	Praetorian cohorts in action at Forum Gallorum; Octavian's cohort destroyed.
36 BC	Praetorian cohorts in Antony's Parthian expedition.
31 BC	Praetorians and *speculatores* in Actium campaign.
30 BC	Octavian disbands Calagurritani bodyguard.
27 BC	Octavian becomes the first Roman emperor; he takes the name Augustus and doubles the praetorians' pay.
13 BC	Praetorian service set at 12 years.
AD 5	Praetorian service increased to 16 years.
AD 9	Varian disaster; *Germani corporis custodes* temporarily removed from Rome.
AD 14	Praetorians and *Germani* with Drusus in Pannonia.
AD 16	Two praetorian cohorts with Germanicus at Idisiovisa.
AD 23	Completion of Castra Praetoria; all nine praetorian cohorts quartered in Rome.
AD 31	Fall of the praetorian prefect Sejanus.
AD 37–47	Number of praetorian cohorts increased to 12.
AD 39	Praetorians and *Germani* in Caligula's German expedition.
AD 41	Caligula murdered by praetorian officers led by Cassius Chaerea; praetorians declare Claudius emperor.
AD 43	Praetorians in Claudius' invasion of Britain.
AD 66–68	Praetorians with Nero in Greece.
AD 68	Praetorians abandon Nero and recognize Galba as emperor; Galba disbands *Germani*.
AD 69	Praetorians declare Otho emperor and kill Galba. Otho's guardsmen campaign against Vitellians in Liguria and Narbonensis; praetorian successes at Placentia and Castores, followed by defeat at Cremona; Otho commits suicide. Vitellius disbands praetorian cohorts and enrols new Guard; Othonian praetorians rally to Flavians; defeat of Vitellians at second battle of Cremona. Last stand of the Vitellian praetorians at the Castra Praetoria.

Guardsmen on the coinage. Top: Caligula addresses the praetorians. The emperor made Cassius Chaerea, a tough praetorian tribune, the butt of offensive jokes, and was killed for it (AD 41). Middle and bottom: coins issued by Gallienus (r. AD 260–268) to celebrate the loyalty of the praetorians and *equites singulares*. Note the lion, perhaps the emblem of the praetorians in the third century AD. (© RHC Archive)

AD 70–76	Praetorian Guard re-formed again, drawing recruits from Othonians, Vitellians and Flavians; cohorts gradually reduced from 19 to nine.
AD 86–87	Praetorian prefect Cornelius Fuscus defeated and killed by Dacians.
AD 89	Praetorians in Domitian's war against the Marcomanni. Number of praetorian cohorts now ten.
AD 97	Praetorians mutiny and execute those involved in murder of Domitian (AD 96).
AD 98	Accession of Trajan. Ringleaders of praetorian mutiny executed; *speculatores* lose special status and probable creation of *equites singulares Augusti*.
AD 101–102 and 105–106	Guardsmen (i.e. praetorians and *equites singulares*) in Trajan's Dacian Wars.
AD 114–117	Guardsmen in Trajan's Parthian War.
AD 121–134	Guardsmen accompany Hadrian on his tours of the provinces.
AD 162–166	Guardsmen in Lucius Verus' Parthian War; returning guardsmen perhaps responsible for bringing plague to Rome.
AD 168–180	Guardsmen in Marcomannic and Sarmatian wars.
AD 188	*Equites singulares* save Commodus from assassination.
AD 193	Praetorians murder Pertinax and auction imperial throne to Didius Julianus. Septimius Severus disbands the Praetorian Guard and immediately re-forms it with soldiers selected from his legions.
AD 197	Praetorians at battle of Lugdunum.
AD 208–211	Praetorians with Severus in Britain.
AD 216–217	Guardsmen in Parthian War.
AD 217	Praetorian *evocatus* murders Caracalla; praetorian prefect Macrinus declared emperor.
AD 218	Praetorians fight for Macrinus against Elagabalus.
AD 222	Emperor Elagabalus murdered by praetorians.
AD 235	Praetorians abandon Emperor Severus Alexander.
AD 238	Legionaries of *II Parthica* and praetorians murder Emperor Maximinus at Aquileia; praetorians kill senatorial emperors Pupienus and Balbinus at Rome and make Gordian III emperor.
AD 243–244	Praetorian prefect Timesitheus defeats Persians at Rhesaina; Gordian III invades Persia but is defeated at Meshike; praetorian prefect Philip declared emperor.
AD 245	Praetorians in Philip's war against the Carpi.
AD 248	Praetorians declare for Decius and murder Philip's son.
AD 260–268	Guardsmen honoured for faithfulness on coinage of Emperor Gallienus.
AD 268	Guardsmen with Gallienus at siege of Mediolanum.
AD 272	Praetorians involved in defeat of Palmyrenes at Emesa.
AD 282	Probus killed in mutiny stirred up by praetorian prefect Carus; guardsmen in Carus' Persian War.
AD 284	Praetorian prefect Aper poisons Emperor Numerian; Diocles, commander of the *protectores*, kills Aper and

	is declared emperor; he takes the name Diocletian.
AD 293	Diocletian instigates Tetrarchy; guardsmen are divided between the four emperors, but praetorians and *equites singulares* maintain their bases in Rome.
AD 297–299	Guardsmen in Galerius' Persian War.
AD 303	Diocletian's praetorians involved in violent persecution of Christians.
AD 306	Constantine recognized as emperor by guardsmen of his father, Constantius I. Maxentius is declared emperor in Rome by Praetorian Guard; he sets about restoring the size of the cohorts.
AD 312	Constantine defeats Maxentius at the battle of the Milvian Bridge; last stand of the Praetorian Guard.
AD 313	Emperor Licinius defeats his rival Maximinus Daia (a former *scutarius* and *protector*) near Adrianople.
AD 324	Constantine defeats Licinius at Chalcedon. *Scholae* guardsmen fight in the campaign.

Constantine the Great. Following his victory at the battle of the Milvian Bridge (AD 312), he disbanded the Praetorian Guard. (© RHC Archive)

ORIGINS AND EARLY HISTORY

Development of the praetorian cohort

In January 62 BC, the small army of the rebel aristocrat Sergius Catiline was brought to battle by the forces of the Roman Republic at Pistoria. Only the core of Catiline's army, a few thousand legionary veterans who had fought

Publius Gessius (centre), the archetypal portrait of a Roman warrior of the age of Caesar, Antony and Octavian. (© ocad123)

for Sulla in the 80s BC, was fully armed. These men put up such a fight that Marcus Petreius, the Republican commander, was forced to call up his praetorian cohort from the reserve. With Petreius leading them, the praetorians charged the centre of Catiline's battle line and the Sullan veterans were finally pushed back. Catiline and his lieutenants were cut down. With its centre broken, Catiline's army finally succumbed to the greater numbers of the enemy. The ill-armed recruits fled, but the Sullan veterans stood their ground until they were all cut down. 'A few in the centre,' wrote Sallust, 'whom the praetorian cohort had scattered, lay a little apart from the rest, but their wounds were all to the front' (*Catiline* 57–61).

When Catiline's rebellion was exposed, the consul Cicero scorned the rebel's principal associates as a *cohors praetoria scortorum*, 'a praetorian cohort of male prostitutes' (*Against Catiline* 2.24). Catiline styled himself *imperator* (supreme commander, general) and as such would normally be accompanied by a *cohors praetoria*, meaning his staff and companions. The praetorian cohort took its name from the *praetorium*, the general's headquarters tent, which in turn derived from *praetor*, the title of the chief magistrate of the Early Roman Republic (in later times the consul replaced the praetor as chief magistrate) (Festus 223L).

Catiline, Cicero and Pompey the Great, who served on the staff of Pompeius Strabo at the siege of Ausculum (90–89 BC), might be described as being part of Strabo's praetorian cohort (*ILS* 8888; Cicero, *Philippics* 12.27), and Julius Caesar's first military post was serving in the *praetorium* of Marcus Thermus, governor of Bithynia, in 81 BC (Suetonius, *Julius* 2).

In some praetorian cohorts the functions of a staff and a bodyguard may have been combined, but while serving as governor of Cilicia in Asia Minor (52 BC), Cicero refers to two distinct praetorian cohorts: his headquarters staff (e.g. Cicero, *Letters to Atticus* 7.2.7) and an elite fighting unit. The latter, however, was not in attendance on the governor. It was acting as the garrison of Epiphaneia, and Cicero reports with great satisfaction that, despite being outnumbered, the cohort, and some *turmae* of cavalry, 'cut to pieces' an invading force of Parthian and Arabian cavalry (*Letters to his Friends* 15.4.7). However, it was unusual for Late Republican commanders to have a praetorian cohort of elite infantry as utilized by Petreius and Cicero. When Julius Caesar parleyed with the German king Ariovistus (58 BC), he selected the Tenth Legion to fulfil temporarily the guard function of a praetorian cohort. Caesar mounted the legionaries on horses and the soldiers joked that they were both a praetorian cohort and *equites*, the upper class of Roman 'knights' who in earlier times had supplied the cavalry arm of the legions (Caesar, *Gallic War* 1.40, 42). The legion proudly recalled this episode by adopting the title *Equestris* (*AE* 1934, 152).

Fighting praetorian cohorts, distinct from the similarly titled groups of staff officers, were essentially *ad hoc* units, recruited at the start of a campaign. Scipio Africanus is credited with the creation of the first *cohors praetoria*, probably in the period 210–202 BC. He selected 'the bravest men' to act as his bodyguards, granted them the status of *immunes* (that is, exempt from fatigues) and made them *sesquiplicarii* ('pay-and-a-half men'); they probably also received a proportionately greater share of booty (Festus 223M). In other Middle Republican armies of the third and second centuries BC, Roman consuls would select guards from the ranks of the *extraoridinarii*, the elite of the Italian *socii* (Allied contingents), and from Roman *evocati*.

Evocati ('the called out') were veterans who had completed the standard term of service but were asked to re-enlist on account of their quality. These guardsmen camped around the *praetorium* and were in constant attendance on the consul 'on the march and on other occasions', presumably meaning in battle (Polybius 6.31.2–3).

Africanus' praetorian cohort probably drew from the best serving legionaries, *evocati* and his clients, all being men of Roman citizen status (cf. the bodyguard formed by his grandson, Scipio Aemilianus, for the Numantine War in 134 BC: Appian, *Spanish Wars* 84). The particular designation of Africanus' guard as a *cohors praetoria* may have been to distinguish it from bodyguards that were mostly composed of non-citizens.

Although they would perform actual and ceremonial guard duties at the *praetorium* and when the army was on the march, praetorians were expected to do more in battle than merely form a protective screen around the general. As Petreius' use of the praetorian cohort at Pistoria demonstrates, praetorians were employed as shock troops.

Cavalrymen and Spanish bodyguards

Despite Africanus' example, not one of the great generals of the Late Republic, namely Marius, Sulla, Pompey or Caesar, is known to have formed a praetorian cohort.

Marius favoured a cavalry guard. It was considered unusual because it was 'formed of the bravest soldiers and not his most intimate friends'. When surprised by Jugurtha and Bocchus in the vicinity of Cirta (106 BC), Marius used the cavalry guard as a roving reserve: 'he went from place to place, now succouring those of his men who were in difficulty, now charging the enemy where they were pressing in greatest numbers' (Sallust, *Jugurtha* 98.1).

Sertorius, the Marian commander in Spain (83/2–81 and 80–73 BC), had such a fanatical bodyguard of Celtiberians (Plutarch, *Sertorius* 14.4–5), that he dismissed his Roman guardsmen (Appian, *Civil Wars* 1.112). It is conceivable that the Romans were a praetorian cohort. Papirius Carbo, a Marian commander in northern Italy, is known to have had a *cohors praetoria* in 82 BC, but it is unclear whether this was his staff or a cohort of guardsmen (Cicero, *Against Verres* 2.1.36).

As we have seen, Caesar was well aware of the bodyguard function of a praetorian cohort, and on one occasion used his favourite legion to fulfil that role. In 45 BC, Caesar travelled through Campania with an escort of 2,000 soldiers, probably drawn from his legions (Cicero, *Letters to Atticus* 13.52.1 – there is no suggestion that these men were not Roman or Italian). Shortly before his assassination in 44 BC, Caesar dismissed a bodyguard of native Spaniards (Suetonius, *Julius* 86; cf. Appian, *Civil Wars* 2.107). There is no evidence of his ever enrolling a formal praetorian cohort.

When Caesar was fighting the Pompeians in Spain in 49 BC, he noted that Marcus Petreius (now a Pompeian general) had a *cohors praetoria caetratorum*, that is, a praetorian cohort of soldiers equipped with the small Spanish *caetra* shield (*Civil War* 1.75). These *caetrati*

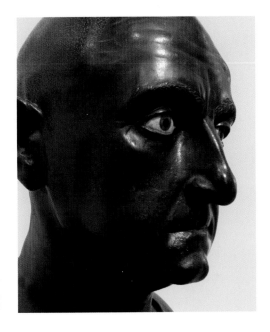

Scipio Africanus (236–183 BC) was the first Roman general to form a praetorian cohort. The guardsmen were selected from veteran legionaries and they received pay and a half, but there are no descriptions of them in action in Scipio's campaigns against Carthage. (© M. Finizio)

Marc Antony, portrayed on a Syrian tetradrachm of 36–33 BC. Antony employed three praetorian cohorts in his Parthian War (36 BC) and by 32–31 BC possessed a *cohors speculatorum*, a 'cohort of scouts'. It probably functioned as a guards unit. (© Gulustan)

were doubtless native Spaniards. Their designation as praetorians might suggest they had been granted Roman citizenship, but it may be that 'praetorian' had become synonymous with 'guardsman', regardless of the citizen status of the actual soldier.

Praetorian guardsmen were therefore something of a rarity before 44 BC, but in the civil war that resulted from Caesar's murder, they became a standard feature of Roman armies.

Antony and Octavian

In the months following Caesar's assassination, Marc Antony (Caesar's chief lieutenant) and Octavian (Caesar's adopted son and heir) manoeuvred for control of the Roman state. They quickly recruited bodyguards from Caesar's legionary veterans. Antony's guard numbered 6,000 men and was commanded by tribunes (Appian, *Civil Wars* 3.5). Appian states that each guardsman had been a centurion, and Antony selected them because of their leadership qualities and experience in warfare. So many centurions could not be found in the whole Roman army, let alone among Caesar's veterans. It seems more likely that the experienced men recruited by Antony were granted the pay and status of centurions. Octavian's guard was even larger – 10,000 men – but it was not subdivided, and marched under a single banner (Appian, *Civil Wars* 3.40). Little is heard of these units after their formations and in October 44 BC, Antony recruited a praetorian cohort from legions recently transferred back to Italy from Macedonia (ibid. 3.45, 52).

At the battle of Forum Gallorum (April 43 BC), Antony's guardsmen were joined by the praetorian cohort of his ally Marcus Lepidus (the praetorians were commanded in the field by Junius Silanus), and together they fought Octavian's own praetorian cohort (derived from his 10,000-strong bodyguard?) until it was destroyed. The praetorian cohort of the consul Aulus Hirtius, under whom Octavian ostensibly served, gave a fine account

A **STANDARD-BEARER OF MARC ANTONY'S *COHORS SPECULATORUM*, 31 BC**
Late Republican guardsmen were picked from veteran legionaries. Here we see a *signifer* (standard-bearer) of Marc Antony's *cohors speculatorum* in the typical mail shirt of a veteran of the Gallic and Civil Wars of 58–40 BC. His iron helmet, taken as plunder from a Gallic warrior, was the inspiration for subsequent legionary helmets. Like later praetorian standard-bearers, the *speculator* wears a lion skin and carries a small *parma* shield. *Speculatores* may have worn a distinctive type of boot (Suetonius, *Caligula* 52), but our standard-bearer's footwear is suggested by the enclosed boots depicted on the gravestone of Minucius Lorarius, a centurion of the *legio Martia*, who died in 43 or 42 BC (*AE* 1982, 395). The *speculator's* standard follows the depiction on the coin issued by Marc Antony to honour his *cohors speculatorum*. The ships' prows suggest the cohort had been involved in a successful naval operation (Crawford 1974, no. 554, 12).
Top: Gallic helmet of Agen-Port type (left), which was adapted by Roman armourers and became the first helmet of the 'Imperial Gallic' series (right).
Bottom: Typical *gladii* and a dagger of the Late Republican and early Augustan periods. The Roman soldiers of this era preferred cut-and-thrust swords with relatively long blades. The dagger was a useful emergency sidearm (Tacitus, *Histories* 4.29). Herodian suggests praetorians habitually carried daggers, even when they were supposed to be unarmed (2.13.10).

Late Republican legionaries and an *eques* on the so-called Altar of Domitius Ahenobarbus. The praetorian cohorts of Antony and Octavian were recruited from veteran legionaries. Note the typical defences of the era – mail shirts and oval *scuta* shields. (© M.-L. Nguyen)

of itself. Reinforced by two cohorts of Octavian's *legio Martia* ('Legion of Mars'), the praetorians held back Antony's complete Second Legion and retreated only when his cavalry threatened to surround them. The praetorians and legionaries made it back to camp with only slight casualties (Cicero, *Letters to his Friends* 10. 30; Appian, *Civil Wars* 3.66–70). After the battle, cavalrymen from Antony's 'bodyguard' searched the field for wounded and carried them to safety (Appian, *Civil Wars* 3.70). It is uncertain whether these cavalrymen were part of the bodyguard recruited in 44 BC, or attached to the praetorian cohort (the Imperial praetorian cohorts had a proportion of mounted men), or if they formed a totally separate cavalry guard.

Antony and Octavian came to terms not long after Forum Gallorum and the subsequent battle at Mutina. They divided the Roman world between themselves and determined to punish Brutus and Cassius, the principal murderers of Caesar. Two engagements were fought against Brutus at Philippi in 42 BC. The first battle was a draw, but Antony's victory in the second engagement was total. His praetorians, probably now organized in several cohorts, can be presumed to have fought in both battles and to have sustained heavy losses. After the battle 8,000 time-served legionaries volunteered to re-enlist and 4,000 of them were gladly accepted by Antony into his praetorian cohorts. The other 4,000 replaced Octavian's praetorian cohort (Appian, *Civil Wars* 5.3). Octavian had enrolled a new cohort of 2,000 men after Forum Gallorum, but it did not reach the fight at Philippi. The transports of his praetorians and *legio Martia* were attacked and sunk by Brutus' navy as they crossed the Adriatic (Appian, *Civil Wars* 4.115; Plutarch, *Brutus* 47.3).

Octavian's new praetorians served with distinction at the siege of Perusia (41–40 BC), defeating an attempted breakout led by Antony's brother, Lucius (Appian, *Civil Wars*, 5.24, 34). It seemed that a full-scale war between Antony and Octavian would result, but their praetorians were instrumental in arranging a reconciliation (ibid. 5.59). Antony then took his praetorians east. Besotted with Cleopatra, queen of Ptolemaic Egypt and former lover of

Caesar, he lingered in his new Egyptian power base for several years before embarking on the long delayed invasion of Parthia (36 BC).

The Parthian War, intended to avenge the great Roman defeat at Carrhae (53 BC), was a disaster, but Antony's praetorian cohorts did perform well when the Parthians occasionally engaged in close combat. (Plutarch, *Antony* 39.2, 5). Octavian capitalized on Antony's defeat and refused to send recruits from Italy to replenish his rival's legions. He was, however, persuaded by his sister Octavia to send Antony a token number of soldiers. Octavia had married Antony in 40 BC, a gesture intended to seal the reconciliation of the warring heirs of Caesar but, besotted with Cleopatra, Antony left Octavia in Italy. Somewhat surprisingly, she remained fiercely loyal to him and in 37 BC arranged for the transfer of 1,000 praetorians (Appian, *Civil Wars*, 5.95). In 35 BC, Octavia herself travelled to Athens with 2,000 chosen men to serve as praetorians in Antony's army, but Antony was not present to receive her and the insult allowed Octavian to present Antony as a faithless adulterer and puppet of a foreign queen (Plutarch, *Antony* 53.2; Dio 49.33.4). By 32 BC Octavian had forced Antony's most influential senatorial supporters from Rome, and then he declared war, not on Roman Antony but on non-Roman Cleopatra.

Antony issued a special series of coins to pay and honour his army. Most of the coins commemorate each of his 23 legions by numeral and title, but also celebrate his praetorian cohorts and a *cohors speculatorum* ('cohort of scouts'). *Speculatores* were associated with, and eventually integrated into, the Imperial praetorian cohorts. The Imperial *speculatores* comprised infantry and cavalry, and acted as close bodyguards to the emperors until

Detail of the 'Nile Mosaic' from Praeneste (Palestrina), showing Late Republican guardsmen taking refreshment. Thought to date to *c.*100 BC, it is interesting that some of the soldiers carry shields with scorpion blazons, a symbol also used by early Imperial praetorians. (© C. Boban)

displaced by the *equites singulares Augusti* at the end of the first century AD. It may be that Antony's *speculatores* performed the functions of scouts (as their title suggests) and bodyguards. The coins commemorating the legions and praetorian cohorts all bear the same motif: an eagle standard flanked by two standards decorated with discs and a crescent. The *cohors speculatorum* coins bear very different standards, decorated with crowns and ships' prows, which may recall a particular success in reconnaissance or fighting at sea (Crawford 1974, no. 544).

It is uncertain how many praetorian cohorts Antony had in 32–31 BC, but Octavian had at least five, which he gave to his admiral Agrippa to serve as marines at the battle of Actium (Orosius, *History Against the Pagans* 6.19.8).

Just before battle was joined at Actium (2 September 31 BC), a grizzled centurion confronted Antony on his flagship. The ship was his floating *praetorium*, suggesting that the centurion was a praetorian or a *speculator*. 'Imperator, why do you despair of these scars of mine and my sword and put your hopes in miserable planks of wood? Give us land,' demanded the centurion, 'for that is where we are accustomed to stand, that is where we conquer our enemies or die' (Plutarch, *Antony* 64.1–2). Antony proceeded to fight at sea, and lost.

Imperial guards

Actium was a scrappy battle but it was certainly decisive. Octavian was the undisputed master of the Roman world. What did the conqueror do with Antony's leaderless and dejected army? Octavian aimed for reconciliation, not retribution. Famous legions, like legio *Equestris*, which had briefly acted as Julius Caesar's praetorian cohort and was acquired by Antony in 43 BC, were enrolled into Octavian's army. The praetorians and *speculatores*, chosen

The remains of Octavian's victory monument overlooking Actium and the Gulf of Ambracia, scene of his decisive victory over Antony and Cleopatra in 31 BC. Octavian's praetorians served as marines in the battle. (© Dan Diffendale)

In AD 23, the praetorian cohorts were quartered together for the first time in a new fortress, the Castra Praetoria. The photo shows the main gate in the north wall; it was engulfed by extensions to the height of the wall in the third and early fourth centuries AD. (© J. van Rooden)

from the best soldiers of these veteran legions, were also welcomed; the nine cohorts of Augustus' Praetorian Guard (a convenient modern title, it was never used by the Romans) might reflect the combined number of praetorian cohorts in 31–30 BC (for the number of cohorts see Keppie 2000, 105; there were certainly nine in AD 23: Tacitus, *Annals* 4.5).

Octavian did disband his personal bodyguard of Calagurritani (Spaniards) after Actium. We know nothing of its role in the war against Antony. Despite having so many praetorians and *speculatores*, Octavian clearly felt the need for more security and at some point acquired a band of German *custodes* (Suetonius, *Augustus* 49.1). The German bodyguard, known as the *Germani corporis custodes* or Batavi (the name of one of the tribes they were recruited from), appears to have shared close protection duties with the praetorian *speculatores*.

In 27 BC, Octavian effectively became the first Roman emperor and was known thereafter as Augustus but, posing as the restorer of the Republic and unwilling to be seen as a military tyrant, he never allowed more than three praetorian cohorts to be in Rome, and these did not have a permanent camp. The six other cohorts were quartered in towns near Rome or elsewhere in Italy. It was not until AD 23 that all of the praetorian cohorts and *speculatores* were quartered together in a single fortress on the outskirts of Rome, the Castra Praetoria (Suetonius, *Augustus* 49.1; *Tiberius* 37.1; Tacitus, *Annals* 4.2.1–2).

The praetorian cohort was developed to provide generals with an elite guard and corps of shock troops, but in the first century of the Empire, praetorians, *speculatores* and *Germani corporis custodes* settled down to life in Rome and were principally concerned with the security of the emperor and his family, performing ceremonial duties and policing (see below). The image of guardsmen as being lazy, undrilled, unfit, overpaid and rarely, if ever, going to war, became an established literary *topos* (Tacitus, *Annals* 1.17.6; *Histories* 1.23), but it is grossly exaggerated. Despite their duties in Rome, Imperial guardsmen remained the fighting elite.

Septimius Valerinus, a legionary transferred to the Praetorian Guard in the third century AD. Note the rope-like pattern on the shaft of his *pilum*. *Notizie degli Scavi* 1923, 391. (*Notizie degli Scavi*)

RECRUITMENT AND TERMS OF SERVICE

From veterans to raw recruits

The guardsmen of the Late Republic, as we have seen, were recruited from the best legionaries and veterans, experienced men who were proven in battle. During Augustus' reign (27 BC to AD 14), the direct recruitment of young men of good family into the praetorians and *speculatores* became the norm. There were two notable exceptions to this general rule. Following the disbandment of Otho's praetorian cohorts in AD 69, the emperor Vitellius enrolled no fewer than 16 cohorts from the legions, and perhaps also auxiliary units, of the German provinces (Tacitus, *Histories* 2.67, 2.93–94). In AD 193, Septimius Severus disbanded the Praetorian Guard for its role in the murder of the emperor Pertinax and the subsequent 'auction' of the Imperial throne to Didius Julianus (Dio 74.1.1–2; Herodian 2.13; Historia Augusta, *Severus* 6.11–7.1, 17.5). Severus immediately began the reconstitution of the praetorian cohorts from the best of his legionaries (Herodian 2.14.5).

The soldiers dismissed by Vitellius were mostly Italians. When discussing the state of the Roman Army in AD 23, Tacitus states that the praetorians were 'mostly chosen from Etruria, Umbria, or from Old Latium and the ancient Roman colonies [in Italy]' (*Annals* 4.5.3). Inscriptions, mostly epitaphs, demonstrate that in the Augustan era praetorian recruits were also being drawn from the north of Italy (Keppie 2000, 116) and, during the course of the first century AD, provincials from areas as distant as Thrace, Pannonia and Germany were admitted into the cohorts (Passerini 1939, 156–159). Other provincials gained ground in the second century AD (see Dio quote, below), but inscribed lists of praetorian veterans show that the makeup of the cohorts remained predominantly Italian until AD 193.

Gravestone of Titus Veratius. As a *speculator praetorianorum*, Veratius belonged to the elite corps that acted as the emperor's bodyguards in the period before AD 98 (*CIL* XI 5388). (© B. Werner)

Speculatores were recruited from the same, mostly Italian, sources but, in the period before AD 98, entry requirements may have been more stringent because of their close protection duties (Suetonius, *Claudius* 35.1; Tacitus, *Histories* 2.11, 33). Some guardsmen began their careers as regular praetorians and later gained promotion to the *speculatores* (*AE* 1991, 794).

The senator Dio, a witness to the disbanding of the praetorians in AD 193, reports:

> Some found fault with him [Septimius Severus] particularly because he abolished the practice of recruiting the Guard exclusively from Italy, Spain, Macedonia and Noricum (a policy that furnished men of more respectable appearance and of simpler habits), and ordered that any vacancies should be filled from all the legions alike. Now he did this with the idea that he should have guards with a better knowledge of the soldier's duties, and should also be offering a kind of prize for those who proved brave in war. But, as a matter of fact, it became only too apparent that he had incidentally ruined the youth of Italy, who turned to brigandage and gladiatorial fighting in place of their former service in the army, and in filling Rome with a throng of motley soldiers most savage in appearance, most terrifying in speech, and most boorish in conversation. (Dio 74.2.3–6)

Discharge diploma of Braetius Iustinus of Mantua, a rare example of an Italian in the Praetorian Guard of the third century AD (*CIL* XVI 153, AD 248). (© RHC Archive)

Dio exaggerates. The three urban cohorts (Rome's paramilitary police force) continued to draw on the manpower of Italy, and Italians formed a significant element in Severus' new legion, *II Parthica*. It did not take long for the praetorian cohorts to revert to the usual method of direct recruitment. The majority of career inscriptions relating to praetorians of the period following AD 193 indicate direct recruitment with no previous military service. A trickle of legionary transfers did continue until the final dissolution of the cohorts in AD 312, but the direct recruits came from the same provincial sources as the legionaries, many of them being the sons of legionaries or relations of guardsmen in Rome. With the gates thrown open to provincials (with Thracians, Pannonians and Moesians supplying no less than two-thirds of recruits), there were few opportunities left for Italians to gain entry into the praetorian cohorts (Passerini 1939, 173–180; but it was not impossible for Italians to join the Guard: *CIL* XVI 153, a praetorian from Mantua discharged in AD 248).

Gravestone of Indus, a Batavian who served in Nero's *Germani corporis custodes*. He died aged 40 (*AE* 1952, 148). (© S. Falco)

The *Germani corporis custodes* may have originated as a band of proven warriors selected by Augustus from German auxiliaries and allied troops, but under his successors the unit was maintained by teenaged recruits with no (obvious) prior military experience. An emperor himself might occasionally go to the German frontier to pick new recruits (e.g. Suetonius, *Caligula* 43), but candidates were probably identified by provincial officers when they applied to join Batavian and other units of Germanic *auxilia* (Dio 55.24.7).

The *equites singulares Augusti* maintained the traditions of the Republic. From the institution of the emperor's cavalry guard in *c.* AD 98, the *singulares* were selected from the best non-citizen troopers already serving in the auxiliary cavalry *alae* (Speidel 1994a, 77–79). However, direct recruits (sons or relations of guardsmen, or men from the preferred recruitment areas of Germany, Pannonia, Thrace) appear in the second century AD and are common in the third, but *allecti*, those specially chosen from the *alae*, still contributed to the elite makeup of the unit (*CIL* VI 3191 and 3239a, recording the transfer in the third century AD of troopers from *ala I Claudia Gallorum Capitoniana*). In AD 241, the decurion Iulius Faustus, and 13 other Moesian *equites singulares Augusti*, set up an altar to Sabazius, a god whose cult may have promised devotees an afterlife. Faustus and his comrades reveal they were *conalares*, meaning 'comrades from the same *ala*', namely *ala I Dardanorum* (*ILS* 2189).

Class and age of recruits

The *Germani corporis custodes* and *equites singulares Augusti* were *peregrini*, free-born 'foreigners'. Even though the auxiliary troopers selected for the *equites singulares* were mostly born inside the Empire, they were *peregrini* and did not have Roman citizenship. Auxiliaries usually received that superior status at the completion of service. However, the names of many *equites singulares*, who died before the completion of service, follow the imperial format of *praenomen* (first personal name) and *nomen* (family name). This suggests the guardsmen had already received citizenship from the emperor and taken his name (for example Publius Aelius, if citizenship was granted by Hadrian, or Titus Aelius, if granted by Antoninus Pius). Other guardsmen may have inherited such imperial names and citizenship from soldier fathers.

In the AD 230s, two decades after the extension of Roman citizenship to all free-born inhabitants of the Empire (below), the diplomas issued to veterans of the *equites singulares* (i.e. the inscribed bronze tablets confirming honourable discharge and rights as veterans) still mentioned that the emperor granted Roman citizenship to those veterans who did not already possess it (Speidel 1994b, nos 76, 79). Not all recruits to the Horse Guard were born within the Empire and therefore would not be Roman citizens. Caracalla recruited Goths, whom he called his Leones (Lions), into the *equites singulares* (Speidel 1994, 64–67). A centurion of the Leones caught and killed Iulius Martialis, the praetorian *evocatus* who assassinated Caracalla in AD 217 (Dio 78.5–6). If men like the Leones were not given Roman citizenship upon enlistment or during service, they were guaranteed that status on becoming veterans.

Like legionaries, praetorian guardsmen, whether regular *milites* (infantrymen), *equites* (cavalrymen), or the elite *speculatores*, had to be Roman citizens. In AD 212, the emperor Caracalla extended Roman citizenship to all free inhabitants of the Empire, technically rendering obsolete the distinction between 'foreign' auxiliaries and citizen legionaries and praetorians, but the old military hierarchy with auxiliaries at the bottom, and praetorians at the top, remained. This is exemplified by the extraordinary career of Traianus Mucianus. In the middle of the third century AD, he began his military service in an obscure auxiliary cohort in Illyricum; he somehow secured transfer to *legio II Parthica* and from there was promoted to *cohors VII praetoria*. Considering the upheaval of the period in which Mucianus joined the Roman Army – an era of unceasing civil wars and barbarian invasions – these moves, especially the unusual jump from an auxiliary cohort to a prestigious legion, were most likely rewards for brave deeds in battle. After completing his service (probably 18 years, see below), he was retained as a praetorian *evocatus*, and then promoted through successive senior centurionates. One of the original high-ranking *protectores* (see glossary), Mucianus ultimately commanded legions and governed provinces (*ILS* 9479).

Good birth and family connections could help secure a place in the Guard, but some had to settle for enlistment in the urban cohorts and hope to secure promotion to a praetorian cohort (*ILS* 2080, an urban soldier, transferred to *cohors VI praetoria*, who eventually became a legionary centurion and was decorated by Hadrian during the Bar Kochba revolt of AD 132–135).

Praetorians had to be tall. Herodian describes them as *megistoi*, Greek for 'the biggest' or (physically) 'the greatest' (5.4.8). He also notes that the short-lived Praetorian Guard, formed by the Gordians in AD 238, was recruited from 'the tallest young men' in Carthage; it probably drew on the urban cohort based there (7.6.2–9). *Speculatores*, being the most select of the praetorians (Tacitus, *Histories* 2.12), may have been chosen from those of six Roman feet or more in height (1.77 metres; Vegetius 1.5). Nero's 'Phalanx of Alexander the Great', later renamed *legio I Italica*, was most unusual in being entirely recruited from men who were six feet tall (Suetonius, *Nero* 19.2). Men of imposing height and build were presumably selected for the *Germani* and the *equites singulares*.

The typical direct praetorian recruit, and the auxiliary troopers who went on to become *equites singulares Augusti*, enlisted between the ages of 17 and 20. Considering the preference for *megistoi*, it is curious to find adolescents as praetorian recruits:

Gravestone of Marcus Ulpius Statius of the *equites singulares Augusti*. His name suggests he, or his father, was given Roman citizenship by Marcus Ulpius Traianus – the emperor Trajan (AE 2001, 1751). (© P. Lemaire)

14-year-old Caesius Verus from Pollentia, or 15-year-old Naevius Verus of Suasa in Umbria (*AE* 1990, 896; 1999, 614). Selvinius Iustinus, one of the early direct recruits to the reconstituted Severan cohorts, was aged 15 (*AE* 2004, 319).

There are also some notable examples of older recruits in the praetorian cohorts. Sempronius Flavus died aged 38 after six years' service (*CIL* VI 2473). Marcus Severus, a mounted praetorian *singularis* (bodyguard to a tribune or the praetorian prefect), died aged 30 after only two years of service (*ILS* 9065). It is possible that these men had seen previous military service in a legion or urban cohort, but it would be most unusual in the Roman world not to brag about something as notable as promotion to the Praetorian Guard.

Length of service

The period of service expected of *Germani corporis custodes* is not known. It seems that most *custodes* were recruited at the age of 17 or 18 (*ILS* 1728, 1727; *AE* 1952, 145). Some died in service aged 40 (*ILS* 1720, 1730), which points to over 20 years in the ranks. *Equites singulares Augusti* usually served for 25–26 years (sometimes exceeded); this might include three to seven years' prior service in an auxiliary *ala* (Speidel 1994a, 77, 89–90). Praetorian guardsmen enjoyed shorter terms of service.

In 13 BC, Augustus set praetorian service at 12 years, four years less than the requirement in the legions. In AD 5, the length of praetorian service was increased to 16 years, and legionary service was set at 20 years (Dio 54.25.6, 55.23.1). This was a source of great discontent in the legions, especially as service did not actually end after 20 years: a further five or six years' service *sub vexillo* (under the veterans' banner) was required before honourable

Gravestone of Iulius Gratus, a veteran of the fifth praetorian cohort. He served for 20 years (*AE* 2001, 1750). (© P. Lemaire)

discharge and a pension, or land, was granted (Keppie 2000, 51–52; Tacitus, *Annals* 1.17). However, even during the Augustan period, or the reign of his successor Tiberius (AD 14–37), it is difficult to find examples of praetorians being allowed to retire after 16 years. Caetronius Passer, who was recruited in AD 11, was honourably discharged in the year of the Two Gemini (AD 29) (*ILS* 2028). Epitaphs of Augustan or Tiberian praetorians from Aquileia record men who died, while still serving, with 17 and 18 *stipendia* (paid years of service: *CIL* V 886, *ILS* 2069). Raius Crispinus, of the sixth praetorian cohort, served for 18 years before discharge was granted (*CIL* IX 4121). Crispinus was an orderly to the Caesar Drusus, and may have accompanied the prince on the mission to quell the legionary mutiny in Pannonia in AD 14 (Tacitus, *Annals* 1.24, 30).

It was probably the emperor Gaius, or his successor Claudius, who increased the number of praetorian cohorts to 12 in the period AD 37–47 (Keppie 2000, 109). These cohorts remained in existence until disbanded by Vitellius in AD 69. Some praetorians in the new cohorts served far in excess of the basic 16 years. Valerius Pudens retired to Thrace (perhaps his place of origin), after 20 years in *cohors XII praetoria* (*AE* 1974, 764). Baebius Thalamo, a soldier in the same cohort, served for 21 years. Unlike Pudens, he is not described as a veteran, and he may have died while still in the ranks (*AE* 2008, 262).

Voltigonius Celer completed 12 years in *cohors X praetoria*. He was then 'transferred into the *speculatores*', and served for another 14 years, making for 26 years in total – the equivalent of a full legionary period of service (*AE* 1991, 794). Celer's notably long service probably belongs to the period AD 37–47 to 76–98, from the time of the establishment of praetorian cohorts X–XII, to the period when the *speculatores* still formed a distinct corps.

In the second century AD, evidence for praetorians being discharged after 16 years is plentiful, but the emperors were now in the habit of discharging time-served soldiers every second year, meaning an extra *stipendium* for some (*CIL* VI 32515, men recruited in AD 119–120 and discharged in 136). During the Marcomannic Wars, some praetorians were retained, or volunteered to remain, in service for up to 19 years (*CIL* VI 32522, listing praetorians recruited in AD 153–156 and discharged in 172).

Following Septimius Severus' reconstitution of the praetorian cohorts, inscriptions suggest that service increased to at least 18 years. A clear example is provided by Domitius Valerianus. Born in Aelia Capitolina, the colony established by Hadrian at Jerusalem, he served first in *legio VI Ferrata*, before winning transfer to *cohors X praetoria pia vindex* (the latter titles mean 'loyal, avenging'), perhaps for conspicuous service as a legionary in Severus' Parthian Wars of AD 194–195 and 197–199. In AD 208, after 18 years' total service in the legion and praetorian cohort, Valerianus received his honourable discharge (*ILS* 2103).

In AD 205, after five years' service in the Dacian legion *XIII Gemina*, the soldier Florus was transferred to a praetorian cohort. He progressed steadily through the posts in his century (*tesserarius, optio, signifer*) and in AD 218, or 222, was promoted to the rank of centurion in *legio XXII Primigenia* in Germany. He returned to Rome in AD 238 and took command of a century in a praetorian cohort (*CIL* IX 1609). Having been recruited in AD 200, Florus' initial legionary and praetorian service was at least 18 years. Iulius Iulianus, a direct recruit to *cohors V praetoria pia vindex* between *c.* AD 198 and 204, received his honourable discharge after 18 years (*CIL* VI 2579). But 18 years, whether combined legionary and praetorian service, or praetorian service alone, appears to have been the minimum requirement.

Aurelius Mucianus, a direct recruit, enlisted aged 15 in AD 209 and was still in the ranks when he died aged 45 in AD 239 (*ILS* 2048). Two years later, in AD 241, a group of praetorians from Moesia set up a dedication to the gods. It was probably made in connection with their imminent departure from Rome for the Eastern Frontier and the war against the Sassanid Persians. Listed by seniority of length of service, the dedicants are headed by Aurelius Maior of *cohors VI praetoria*; he has 30 *stipendia* (*CIL* VI 32549). Thirty years would not be unusual for *evocati*, but neither Mucianus nor Maior are distinguished as such.

Cornelius Memor, a Norican who died at the grand old age of 80, is described on his epitaph as a 'former soldier of the fourth praetorian cohort, in the century of Patroilus, he served as a soldier for 28 years'. This length is qualified by *iteratus*, meaning 'a second time' (*ILS* 2050). This may refer to a second period of service as a praetorian *evocatus*.

Evocati

Evocati were time-served guardsmen who, on account of their leadership qualities or technical expertise, were invited to re-enlist in special corps attached to the Praetorian Guard. Like a centurion, the *evocatus* carried a *vitis* (vine stick) as a badge of rank (Dio 55.24.8). When the Praetorian Guard went on campaign, *evocati* provided a core of experienced veterans (Tacitus, *Histories* 2.11, where the 'praetorian veterans' are to be identified as *evocati*).

Some *evocati* were earmarked for promotion to centurionates. In fact, some were fast-tracked to commands over auxiliary units (*RIB* 1896, an *evocatus* made tribune of a British auxiliary cohort in AD 235–238). Other *evocati* were sent out to the legions as training instructors, or retained within the Guard to serve as technical experts.

After completing his initial service in the Praetorian Guard in the middle of the first century AD, Pellartius Celer was retained by an emperor as an *evocatus*, and then made *armidoctor* (senior weapons instructor) of *legio XV Apollinaris*. He clearly put his training methods into practice on the battlefield, for he was decorated by the future emperor Titus with a gold crown for gallantry in the Jewish War; the decoration may have been presented in the ceremony held following the capture of Jerusalem in AD 70 (Josephus, *Jewish War* 7.13–16). After 43 years of service, Celer was eventually discharged by the emperor Domitian, who awarded him a considerable pension (*AE* 1952, 153).

One of the most interesting praetorian *evocati* is Vedennius Moderatus (*ILS* 2034). Originally a legionary of *XVI Gallica* (recruited in AD 59), he appears to have been a member of the detachment of that legion when it fought for the emperor Vitellius at the second battle of Cremona in AD 69. Moderatus' funerary monument is decorated with a detailed relief of a *scorpio* (scorpion) catapult. He may well have been operating one of the artillery machines (*tormenta*) that assailed the ex-Othonian praetorians at Cremona:

Altars set up at forts north of Hadrian's Wall by the tribunes Paternius Maternus and Aurunceius Felicissimus. Both were former praetorian *evocati* and had been promoted directly to the command of auxiliary cohorts in the third century AD (*RIB* 966, 988). Maternus states he was an '*evocatus* of the palace'. (© RHC Archive)

[The Flavian general] Antonius Primus strengthened his wavering line by bringing up the praetorians [the Othonians dismissed by Vitellius]. On engaging they drove back the enemy, only to be driven back themselves, for the Vitellians had concentrated their artillery (*tormenta*) on the raised road that they might have free and open ground from which to fire. Their earlier shots had been scattered and had struck the trees without injuring the enemy. A ballista of enormous size belonging to the Fifteenth Legion began to do great harm to the Flavians' line with the huge stones that it hurled. And it would have caused wide destruction if it had not been for the splendid bravery of two soldiers, who, taking the shields from the dead [Vitellians] and so disguising themselves, cut the ropes and springs of the machine. They were at once run through and thus their names are lost, but there is no doubt about their deed. (Tacitus, *Histories* 3.22).

After Cremona, the defeated Vitellians were dispersed around Illyricum to prevent their rallying in Italy (Tacitus, *Histories* 3.35). It seems, however, that Moderatus' technical expertise was recognized and he was enrolled into Vespasian's Praetorian Guard, which drew on Othonian, Vitellian and Flavian sources. After eight years in *cohors IX praetoria*, he was honourably discharged by Vespasian and then immediately recalled to service as an *evocatus* (AD 77). He served for a further 23 years as *architectus armamentarii imperatoris* (engineer of the emperor's armoury), presumably specializing in artillery, as the *scorpio* catapult relief on his grave altar suggests (Tacitus, *Annals* 12.56.2 for the praetorians' use of artillery). Moderatus was twice decorated, by Vespasian (r. AD 69–79) and Domitian. The circumstances of the award from Vespasian are obscure, but Domitian's German, Dacian and Sarmatian wars would have provided ample opportunities for the *evocatus* to display his artillery skills and prove his worth as a military engineer.

Pay and pension
The praetorians of Scipio Africanus were *sesquiplicarii*, meaning they received one and a half times the basic legionary rate of pay. If this remained the standard into the Late Republican period, Augustus' doubling of praetorian pay in 27 BC (his first act as emperor) meant praetorians earned three times the basic legionary rate (Dio 53.11.1). So much, then, for the claim in the epitaph of Caetronius Passer that he had always lived in honourable poverty (*ILS* 2028). Praetorian under-officers and centurions were presumably paid three times the rates of equivalent ranks in the legions. *Equites singulares Augusti* must have received better pay than their comrades in the *alae*. How much the *Germani corporis custodes* were paid can only be guessed, but they normally received a retirement bonus: '[In AD 68, the emperor Galba] disbanded the cohort of Germans, whom previous Caesars had made their bodyguard and had found absolutely faithful in many emergencies, and sent them back to the native land without any rewards (*commoda*).' (Suetonius, *Galba* 12.2)

Praetorians received a lump sum on retirement, almost twice the amount given to legionaries who had completed more *stipendia* (Dio 55.23.1).

Like other Roman soldiers, Imperial guardsmen were subject to deductions from pay, and a form of institutionalized extortion. Upon the elevation of Otho in AD 69 (the coup was engineered by an enterprising band of *speculatores*), the praetorian rankers demanded:

> The payments usually made to centurions to secure furloughs should be abolished, since they amounted to an annual tax on the common soldiers. A quarter of each maniple would be away on furlough or loafing about the camp itself, provided the soldiers paid the centurion his price, and no one cared how the burden pressed on the soldiers or how they got their money; in reality it was through highway robbery, petty thieving, and by menial occupations that the soldiers purchased rest from military service. Moreover the richest soldiers would be cruelly assigned to the most fatiguing labour until they bought relief. Then, impoverished and demoralised by idleness, the

soldier would return to his maniple poor instead of well-to-do and lazy instead of energetic; so ruined one after another by the same poverty and lack of discipline, they were ready to rush into mutiny and dissension, and finally into civil war. But Otho wished to avoid alienating the centurions by generosity to the common soldiers, and so he promised that the state treasury should pay for the annual furloughs, a procedure which was undoubtedly useful and which later was established by good emperors as a fixed rule of service. (Tacitus, *Histories* 1.46)

The Pisonian Conspiracy of AD 65 involved a number of praetorian of tribunes and centurions. They were appalled by Nero's unmanly theatrical antics, but the bulk of praetorians remained loyal to the emperor and they were rewarded with a distribution of cash and a remission 'of the price of the grain ration previously supplied to them at the market rate' (Tacitus, *Annals* 15.72.2). The *Germani*, whom Nero particularly trusted because they were foreigners, were active in rounding up conspirators (ibid. 15.58.2), and presumably received similar rewards.

TRAINING

In AD 69, the northern Italian city of Placentia was garrisoned by praetorians loyal to the new emperor Otho. But the army of Vitellius, another claimant to the throne, had surrounded the city. Vitellius' soldiers, mostly veteran legionaries and auxiliaries of the German provinces, shouted insults at the praetorian defenders:

They railed at Otho's soldiers, calling them actors, dancers, spectators at Pythian and Olympic games, men who had never seen a campaign or fighting, but thought highly of themselves because they had cut off the head of a defenceless old man [the emperor Galba], but would not openly enter a conflict and battle of men. (Plutarch, *Otho* 6.1)

The praetorians *did* want to fight in the open field (cf. Tacitus, *Histories* 2.18), and so infuriated were they by the Vitellians' insults, that when the assault came, the Vitellians were repulsed with heavy losses and forced to lift the siege (ibid. 2.21–22; Plutarch, *Otho* 6.2).

The Vitellians were more or less correct about the praetorians not having seen battle (it was 26 years since some praetorians had fought in Claudius' invasion of Britain), and they were certainly unskilled in the construction of camps and field works (Tacitus, *Histories* 2.19), but the alacrity with which Otho's praetorians took to combat is striking. Despite their inexperience, Otho's praetorians were victorious in two battles in Liguria (the first against untrained levies, but the second a two-day struggle against Vitellian regulars); they pushed back Vitellian veterans at Placentia and Castores, and more than held their own at the first battle of Cremona (Tacitus, *Histories* 2.12–15, 18–22, 24–26, 44; Wellesley 2000, 81–82 elucidates their role at Cremona). The praetorians were certainly enthused by Otho's leadership. His charisma inspired devotion. He marched alongside the praetorians like a common soldier – unkempt and wearing the plain iron armour of a ranker. But the effect of his leadership went only so far; he was not actually present at any of the battles against the Vitellians (Tactius, *Histories* 2.11; Suetonius, *Otho* 9.1). The successes of his praetorians against Vitellius' veteran troops points to rigorous combat training.

The tribunes who commanded praetorians were all highly experienced officers, men who had served as *primus pilus*, the highest rank of legionary centurion. When Subrius Flavus, a praetorian tribune involved in the Pisonian Conspiracy against Nero (AD 65), was about to be executed, he criticized the soldiers who had dug the pit into which his body was to be flung because it was too shallow. 'Not even this,' he said, 'is in line with your training' (Tacitus, *Annals* 15.67.3–4). One can well imagine the exacting standards of a man like Flavus on the Campus Cohortium, the training ground outside the Castra Praetoria at Rome.

Not long after the construction of the Castra Praetoria, the emperor Tiberius invited the Roman Senate to watch the training exercises of the Guard: 'Tiberius gave the senators an exhibition of the praetorians at drill, as if they were ignorant of the power of these troops. His purpose was to make them more afraid of him, when they saw his defenders to be so numerous and so strong.' (Dio 57.24.5)

Emperor Otho. His charisma inspired great devotion in the praetorians, but he never led them into battle. (© M. Harrsch)

It should be remembered that many senators had served as legionary tribunes and commanders; they would know well-trained soldiers when they saw them. The emperors would inspect the praetorians' drill (e.g. Caligula: Dio 59.2.1), and members of the Imperial family might even participate (e.g. the young Nero: Suetonius, *Nero* 7.2), which would certainly encourage officers and rankers to strive for excellence. As a former legionary officer of unusually extensive experience, the emperor Hadrian (r. AD 117–138) was a particular stickler. 'He kept the soldiers in training as if war were imminent' (Historia Augusta, *Hadrian* 10.2), and 'drilled the men in every kind of battle' (Dio 69.9.3). For cavalry guardsmen this meant practising the lance and bow fighting techniques of the principal mounted enemies of Rome – the Parthians and Sarmatians (Arrian, *Tactica* 44).

Training instructors

As masters of the *armatura* (below) and as the men who led the centuries and *turmae* of the guards units into battle, centurions and decurions played a major role in the training of recruits and overseeing the daily drill of the regulars (Vegetius 2.14, 23; Josephus, *Jewish War* 3.73; Cowan 2003, 11–12 for an outline of Roman basic training). Some decurions, and even commanders, of the *Germani corporis custodes* were recruited from gladiators, doubtless chosen because of their skill with weapons (below). The guards units also possessed a range of specialist training officers.

Praetorians with the rank of *armatura* were presumably responsible for teaching the drill of the same name (*CIL* VI 2699; *ILS* 9070, a trainee *armatura*). This special weapons drill was much admired by Vegetius because those who mastered it could outfight any other soldiers (1.13). Unfortunately, the *armatura* is nowhere clearly described, but Vegetius tells us 'a centurion is chosen for great strength and tall stature, as a man who hurls spears and

Maximinus, the horse guardsman who became emperor in AD 235.
(© M.-L. Nguyen)

javelins skilfully and strongly, has expert knowledge of how to fight with the sword and rotate his shield and has learned the whole art of *armatura*' (2.14).

More senior training instructors in the praetorian cohorts and *equites singulares Augusti* were called *doctores* (teacher, instructor) and *campidoctores* (field instructors). Some were probably responsible for directing tactical manoeuvres of centuries and cohorts, such as deploying into battle lines, practising formations like the *testudo*, and fighting mock battles. It may be that practice in battle formations and manoeuvres occurred three times per month (Vegetius 1.27). Other *doctores* were specialists in particular weapons and fighting techniques, like archery (*CIL* VI 3595). Aurelius Maior, a native of Carthage, died aged 56 in the post of 'salaried archer of *legio II Parthica*' at Albanum (*CIL* VI 37262). The reference to salary (*salarium*) indicates that Maior was an *evocatus*; ordinary soldiers received *stipendia*. He presumably served as the legion's archery instructor. The legion seems to have been unique in possessing archers. An unpublished gravestone from Apamea in Syria identifies Aurelius Titus, a legionary of *II Parthica* with 23 years' service, as *immunis sagiattarius*, 'archer, with immunity from fatigues'. Titus' gravestone gives *II Parthica* the honorific title *Severiana*, and so places his death during the Persian War of the emperor Severus Alexander (AD 231–233).

That *doctores* were junior to *campidoctores* is shown by a dedication made to Nemesis of the Parade Ground by Aelius Pacatus, on his promotion from *doctor* to *campidoctor* of the first praetorian cohort (*ILS* 2088). *Campidoctores* were men of considerable military service. Aurelius Eliaseir began his army career in an unspecified legion. After ten years, he was promoted to the Guard, and remained there for a quarter of a century, retiring (or dying) with the rank of *campidoctor* of the ninth praetorian cohort. Despite his long service, he does not appear to have been an *evocatus* (*CIL* VI 2697).

Doctores and *campidoctores* were also found in the *equites singulares Augusti* (*doctor*: *CIL* VI 3239a; a possible archery *campidoctor*: *CIL* VI 31150, with Speidel 1994b, no. 14). The praetorian cavalry were drilled by *campidoctores* (*AE* 1957, 296), but the most important cavalry instructors of the Guards units were the *exercitatores* (exercisers). They were of senior

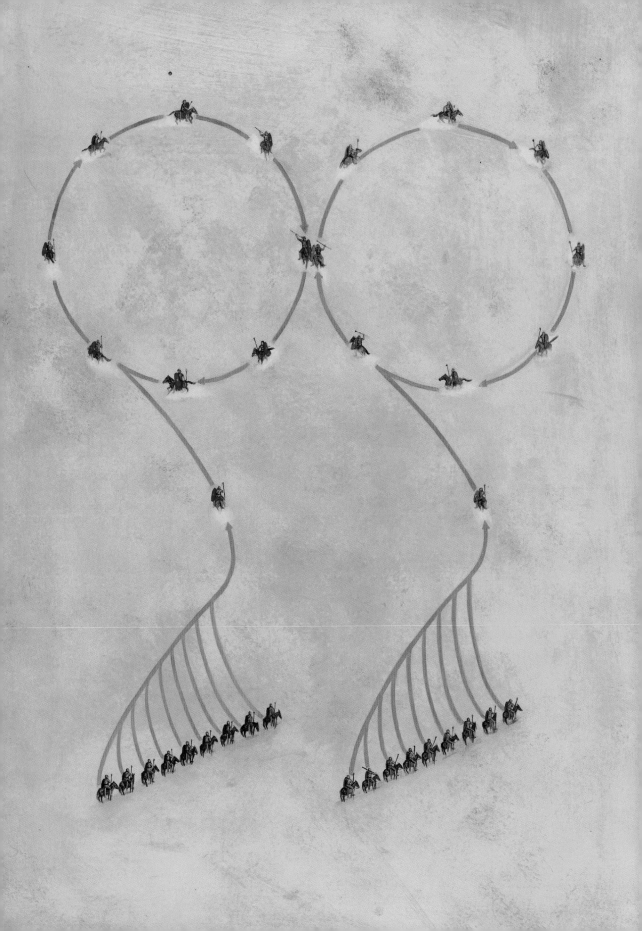

centurial rank and second only to the tribunes in charge of the praetorian cohorts and *equites singulares* (*CIL* X 1127; VI 31150). When the *speculatores* still formed a distinct corps, their cavalry element was trained by a *centurio exercitator*.

Vettius Valens served as *centurio exercitator equitum speculatorum* in the mid-first century AD (*ILS* 2648). He must have been well educated, and his family probably had good political connections, because his first post in the Praetorian Guard was as clerk to the praetorian prefect. He saw action in Claudius' invasion of Britain (AD 43) and was decorated for valour. After completing his service in *cohors VIII praetoria*, he became an *evocatus* and was decorated for a second time (the circumstances of the award are not known). Promotion to centurionates in Rome soon followed – in the *vigiles*, *statores* (a corps of messengers associated with the praetorians), urban and praetorian cohorts, and then as *centurio exercitator* of the cavalry of the *speculatores*. This was the springboard for promotion to senior centurionates in the legions; as *primus pilus* of *legio VI Victrix* in Spain he was decorated for a third time, on account of his 'successful deeds against the Astures'. In AD 66, following promotion to the equestrian order and various commands as a tribune (including *cohors III praetoria*), he was the procurator of the Spanish province of Lusitania, a high official with civil and military powers.

The future emperor Maximinus (r. AD 235–238) was transferred from an auxiliary *ala* to the enlarged Horse Guard of Septimius Severus (cf. Historia Augusta, *Two Maximini* 2–3). He rose to become a decurion of the *equites singulares* Augusti and perhaps even one of the unit's *exercitatores* (Speidel 1994a, 69). Guardsmen could certainly go far!

Exercitatores led by example in battle. Caesernius Senecio, *exercitator* of the praetorian horse, appears to have been killed during Septimius Severus' British War (AD 208–211). Senecio's body was brought back to Rome for burial by his freedman (*ILS* 2089). The gravestone of an *exercitator* of the *equites singulares Augusti* killed during the third century AD, proudly declares 'he died fighting for the Republic' (Speidel 1994b, no. 756).

ORGANIZATION

Praetorian cohorts

Literary and epigraphic sources indicate that Augustus had nine praetorian cohorts, though the number may actually have fluctuated during his reign (Passerini 1939, 44–53). Nine cohorts were maintained by Tiberius in AD 23 (Tacitus, *Annals* 4.5), and this number almost certainly reflects the late Augustan size of the Guard. Command of individual cohorts was given to tribunes, equestrian officers who had previously served as senior legionary centurions. In 2 BC, Augustus placed all of the cohorts under the control of two praetorian prefects (sometimes there was only one), and thus created the most senior equestrian posts in the Empire (Keppie 2000, 111–111). The prefects might lead the cohorts into battle, sometimes disastrously: in AD 86 or 87, the praetorian prefect Cornelius Fuscus was killed and defeated by the Dacians (Suetonius, *Domitian* 6.1; Dio 67.6.5–6). They would accompany the emperor when he was on campaign, but the prefects increasingly functioned as senior ministers of state, with great administrative and legal responsibilities.

The number of cohorts was increased to 12 by Gaius-Caligula or Claudius (above). In AD 69, the emperor Vitellius disbanded the 12 Othonian cohorts (he did, however, grant the soldiers honourable discharge), and formed 16 new milliary cohorts drawn from his own legions (Tacitus, *Histories* 2.67, 93–94; Suetonius, *Vitellius* 10.1). Tacitus emphasizes the milliary (thousand-strong) size of Vitellius' cohorts and this suggests that, from the time of Augustus to Otho, the cohorts had been quingenary – each 500 men strong, the norm for the period. However, Vitellius' cohorts were probably milliary only on paper; withdrawing 16,000 men from the legions, and even auxiliary units, would have wiped out much of his field army. There is no suggestion that Vitellius' legions were under strength or full of new recruits at the second battle of Cremona. In fact, Vitellius' praetorians were not involved in the battle.

Flavius Vespasian, the victor of the civil war of AD 69, found himself in possession of a huge number of praetorians: former Othian praetorians to whom he had promised restoration of rank; the surviving Vitellians, who were keen to maintain their elevated status; and Flavian legionaries who expected to be rewarded for their services (Tacitus, *Histories* 2.67, 82; 4.2). In AD 70, the Flavian general Licinius Mucianus began the process of whittling down the numbers:

Those who had been dismissed by Vitellius and had then banded together to support Vitellius now asked to be restored to service in the praetorian cohorts; and the legionaries selected with the same prospect demanded the pay promised to them. Even the Vitellians could not be removed without much bloodshed, but it would cost an enormous sum to keep such a great force of men under arms. Mucianus entered the camp [Castra Praetoria] to examine more closely the length of each man's service. He drew up the victors with their proper insignia and arms... Then the Vitellians, whose surrender at Bovillae I have mentioned [4.2], and all the others who had been rounded up in the capital and its suburbs, were led into the parade ground in rags. Mucianus ordered them to march to one side, and directed that the soldiers from Germany and Britain and all the troops there were among them from other armies should take positions by themselves. They were paralysed by the first sight of their situation, when they beheld opposite them what seemed to them like an enemy's battle line, threatening them with weapons and defensive arms, while they were themselves hemmed in, unprotected, squalid and filthy; then, when they began to be divided and marched in different directions, all were smitten with horror; the soldiers from Germany were the most terrified, for they thought that by this division they were being marked for slaughter. They began to throw themselves on the breasts of their fellow-soldiers, to hang on their necks, to beg for a farewell kiss, praying them not to desert them or allow them to suffer a different fate when their cause had been the same; they kept appealing now to Mucianus, now to the absent emperor, finally to heaven and the gods, until Mucianus stopped their needless panic by calling them all 'soldiers bound by the same oath' and 'soldiers of the same emperor.' He was the readier to do this as the victorious troops by their cheers seconded the tears of the others. Thus the day ended. But a few days later, when Domitian [Vespasian's son] addressed them, they received him with recovered confidence: they treated with scorn the offers of lands but asked for service in the army and pay. They resorted to appeals, it is true, but to appeals that

The emperor Vitellius. He disbanded the 12 Othonian praetorian cohorts and replaced them with 16 milliary cohorts drawn from his legions. (© W. Sauber)

Fragments from the Temple of the Flavians at Rome, showing Vespasian (centre, being crowned by Victory) and one of his praetorians (left). By AD 76, Vespasian had reduced the number of praetorian cohorts to nine. His son, Domitian, who built the Temple, increased the number to ten. (© C. Seeman)

admitted no denial; accordingly they were received into the praetorian camp, then those whose age and length of service warranted it were honourably discharged. Others were dismissed for some fault or other, but gradually and one at a time, the safest remedy for breaking up a united mob. (Tacitus, *Histories* 4.46)

This 'mob' amounted to at least 19 cohorts (*AE* 1995, 227), but by AD 76 the number had been reduced to the Augustan establishment of nine (*CIL* XVI 21). Domitian added a tenth praetorian cohort (*CIL* XVI 81, AD 89), and this remained the establishment as late as AD 306, just six years before the final dissolution of the Guard (*RMD* 78).

The Flavian cohorts were most likely 1,000 strong. Hyginus' *Liber de Munitionibus Castrorum* (*Book About Camp Fortifications*), which may date to the late first or second centuries AD, notes that praetorian cohorts required double the space in camp because they had larger tents than the legionaries (6). Rather than suggest more space accorded to a more prestigious unit, it probably shows that the praetorians were organized into milliary cohorts (most legionary cohorts were quingenary). The cohorts were certainly milliary in the Severan era, AD 193–235 (Dio 55.24.6, retrojecting the strength of the Severan cohorts onto the Augustan era), and probably remained so until the late third century AD.

It should be noted here that because Roman military *centuria* ('century' sub-units) numbered 80 men (Hyginus, *de Munitionibus Castrorum* 1), and because each praetorian cohort had six double-sized *centuriae*, the actual optimum size of a milliary cohort was 960 men.

The basic internal organization of the praetorian cohort was the same as the legionary cohort. Each cohort was divided into six centuries (*CIL* VI 32515, 32520). A century was commanded by a centurion, aided, in order of seniority, by a *signifer* (standard-bearer), *optio* (centurion's deputy) and *tesserarius*, the under-officer responsible for distributing the daily watchword (*CIL* II 2610 for the hierarchy within the century). The century also required a horn-player (*cornicen*) or trumpeter (*bucinator*) to sound the signals on the parade ground and in battle (*CIL* VI 2752, *ILS* 2064).

Praetorian cavalry

The praetorian cavalrymen of a particular cohort were enrolled into the centuries, but formed a separate fighting unit (Tacitus, *Histories* 2.11, 24). It is not known whether the cavalrymen were included in the strength of the century, or whether they were supernumeraries. A passage in Hyginus' *de Munitionibus Castrorum* (30) indicates there were at least 400 praetorian troopers. They accompany four praetorian cohorts.

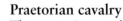

At first sight, this suggests 100 cavalry per cohort, but when Drusus went to negotiate with legionary mutineers in Pannonia in AD 14, he was escorted by two praetorian cohorts (specially reinforced, probably by drafts from the seven other cohorts, *speculatores* and *evocati*) and 'the greater part of the praetorian cavalry and the flower of the *Germani* [*corporis custodes*]' (Tacitus, *Annals* 1.24.1–2). This could suggest that it was normal for the bulk of the praetorian cavalry to go out on campaign, even if only a few praetorian cohorts were involved.

The praetorian cavalry had its own *vexillum* (banner). The *vexillarius* (banner-bearer) outranked the cavalry *optio* (ILS 9190), but it is not clear to whom these under-officers answered. As we have seen, the cavalrymen were carried on the books of the centuries, and the cavalrymen were not organized into *turmae*. Tacitus does mention *turmae* of praetorians but in the general sense of cavalry, just as he uses the old-fashioned term maniple (not a tactical sub-unit since the second century BC) to refer to small bodies of infantry. In AD 52, the emperor Claudius arranged a great spectacle on the Fucine Lake – a naval battle to be fought by criminals. Praetorian infantry and cavalry provided security: 'He equipped triremes, quadriremes, and 19,000 combatants. The lists he surrounded with rafts, so as to leave unauthorised points of escape… On the rafts were stationed maniples and *turmae* of the praetorian cohorts, covered by a breastwork from which to operate their catapults and ballistas… The battle, though one of criminals, was contested with the spirit and courage of free men, and, after much blood had flowed, the combatants were exempted from destruction.' (Tacitus, *Annals* 12.56.2–3)

The *centuriones exercitatores* were certainly of high enough rank to command elements of the praetorian cavalry, but not the full complement. During wars of Domitian, or perhaps in the reign of Trajan (AD 98–117), the praetorian cavalry was commanded in the field by Arruntius Claudianus, an experienced equestrian officer from Lycia (AE 1972, 572). During his tenure, Claudianus won an array of decorations, suggesting he and the praetorian troopers saw extensive action.

Sulpicius Peregrinus, a mounted *speculator* of the first century AD (*AE* 1955, 24). His curious 'lance' has a vaguely heart-shaped head pointing towards the ground, and a small block or roundel at the other end. It has been suggested the block was used to push back spectators who got too close to the emperor. (© Duncan B. Campbell)

Speculatores

In December AD 76, new veterans of the Praetorian Guard were presented with bronze diplomas. These documents provided evidence of their 'courageous and loyal military service' and confirmed their right of *conubium* (marriage) with non-citizen women: children from such unions would be recognized as Roman citizens. The seniority of the *speculatores* in the praetorian hierarchy is emphasized: 'I, Emperor Caesar Vespasian Augustus… append the names of those *speculatores* who served in my *praetorium*, and also the soldiers who served in the nine praetorian cohorts' (*ILS* 1993).

The seniority of the *speculatores* would not last for much longer. By AD 98, if not during the reign of Domitian, they were superseded by the *equites singulares Augusti*, and like the praetorian *equites*, *speculatores* were thereafter enrolled into the centuries of the praetorian cohorts.

The organization of the *speculatores* prior to their full integration into the praetorian cohorts is not clear. The corps comprised both infantry and cavalry (*CIL* V 45; *AE* 1954, 162). We have already encountered the *exercitator* of the mounted *speculatores*. Other centurions are known: the *centurio speculatorum* and the *centurio speculatorum equitum*, concerned the infantry and cavalry elements (*ILS* 2020; *CIL* V 7164). It is not certain whether the *exercitator* outranked these centurions. Any grade of *speculator* centurion was evidently senior to the centurions of the praetorian cohorts but, supposing the *speculatores* had a strength equivalent to a regular quingenary cohort (480–500 men), as is suggested by Marc Antony's *cohors speculatorum*, it would have required a commander of equestrian rank, like the tribunes of the regular praetorian cohorts. No such officer is known.

It has been suggested that a senior centurion of Guard, bearing the title of *centurio trecenarius* commanded the *speculatores* and, further, that his title points to the corps of *speculatores* being 300 strong. It is conceivable that a centurion could command up to 300 men or a triple-sized century; from the Severan period, the centuries of the urban cohorts appear to have been 250 strong (Dio 55.24.6; the centuries were probably 240 strong, triple the standard complement of 80 men). However, the most likely explanation of *trecenarius*, is that it was an honorific title applied to men who had passed through three of the Rome centurionates – usually in the cohorts of the *vigiles*, urban troops and praetorians (Mann 1983).

Just as there is no evidence for a commander (apart from the emperor!) of the *speculatores*, there is no sign of organization into typical Roman tactical sub-units like centuries, *turmae* or *decuriae*. When the *speculatores* ceased to form a special bodyguard, they were enrolled into the cohorts and, like all other praetorians, identified themselves by cohort numeral and the name of their centurion. It may be that they still formed a distinct fighting unit but, unlike the praetorian cavalry, there is no evidence for the *speculatores* having their own standard or under-officers like *optiones*. The function of the *speculatores* in the period following AD 98 is uncertain. They were perhaps still concerned with scouting and reconnaissance or, considering their reputation in the first century AD as chosen men, they may have formed the leading ranks in battle formations.

It is worth noting that the *laterculi*, the inscribed lists of praetorian veterans of the second and early third centuries AD, contain far more *speculatores* than *equites*, but it is uncertain whether some of the *speculatores* still fought from horseback. Ulpius Emeritus, a praetorian of the third century AD, is described on his gravestone as *miles speculator* (*CIL* VI 2543). The use of *miles* might be to distinguish him from other *speculatores* who were *equites* (cavalrymen), but *miles* is probably used in the general sense of 'soldier' and not the more specific meaning of 'infantryman'.

In AD 227, a group of praetorians from Philippolis in Thrace made a dedication to the god Asclepius. One of the dedicants was a *speculator*: Aurelius Diogenes of the seventh praetorian cohort, in the century of Quartus (*CIL* VI 32543). There are many epitaphs of praetorian *speculatores* that can be assigned to the third century AD, but Diogenes is the last precisely dated example.

It has been suggested that *speculatores* did not disappear in the middle years of the third century AD, but acquired a new title: *tectores*. In Latin, *tector* means plasterer, but the military grade was probably an abbreviated form of *protector* (*AE* 1974, 648, a *protector* in *legio II Parthica*). We know of two praetorian examples, both *tectores equitum*, that is mounted 'bodyguards' (*CIL* VI 2773 and *ILS* 2090, who was also a priest of the temple of Mars in the Castra Praetoria). However, it is not easy to determine whether *tector* was a new type of *speculator*, or whether it was an alternative title for the *singularis* who guarded praetorian tribunes and prefects (*ILS* 2074, 2080).

Germani Corporis Custodes

The size and organization of the German Bodyguard is better understood. The unit was organized as cohort (Suetonius, *Galba* 12.2), probably of *c.* 500 men. The *Germani* could fight on foot or from horseback and were organized into *decuriae* (cf. Tacitus, *Annals* 15.58.2 for them operating as cavalry).

Gravestone of Marius Alexander, a *decurio* of the *equites singulares Augusti*. He joined the Horse Guard (or an *ala*) at 14 and died, still in the ranks, aged 40. At the bottom of the memorial, a groom is shown with the *turma* commander's remounts (*AE* 1982, 76). (© R. Benôit)

OVERLEAF LEFT The only known depiction of a standard-bearer of the *equites singulares Augusti*. The *signifer* wears the *paenula*, an all-weather military cloak. His bushy beard and hairstyle, the fashion favoured by Hadrian and the Antonine emperors, dates the memorial to the second century AD. (© Florian Himmler)

OVERLEAF RIGHT Detail of the standard of the *equites singulares Augusti*. Interestingly, it follows the form of an infantry standard and the eroded mural crown decoration (second from top), demonstrates that the horse guardsman had fought on foot in the capture of a fortress or city. (© Florian Himmler)

The *decuria* was a traditional Roman cavalry sub-unit of ten men, but the *decuriae* of the *Germani* were perhaps three times that size. Each sub-unit was led by a *decurio*, with an *optio* as his second in command (*AE* 1952, 146). Caligula and Nero chose some of their decurions not from the German recruitment grounds, but from the gladiatorial arenas. Some, like Sabinus, who hunted down the praetorian murderers of Caligula, or Nero's favourite Spiculus, rose to command the bodyguard (Josephus, *Jewish Antiquities* 19.122; Dio 60.28.2; Suetonius, *Nero* 30.2).

C VETERAN HORSE GUARDSMAN, EARLY FOURTH CENTURY AD

This veteran *eques singularis* is dressed in the fashion of the early fourth century AD, but he retains equipment dating to the third century AD. Legionaries seem to have given up ring-buckle belts by the AD 280s, but the gravestone of the so-called Castel Sant'Angelo praetorian, dated to AD 293–305, shows the deceased wearing a military belt with a large ring-buckle (Rocchetti 1967–68). A gravestone of an *eques singularis* at Salo, who may have been among the Maxentian cavalry killed nearby at Brixia in AD 312, also shows the deceased wearing a ring-buckle belt, while a servant holds up his eagle-crested helmet (Speidel 1994b, no. 620). Such helmets had a separate face guard (see inset **2**). A more typical helmet of the period was the 'spangenhelm', composed of rivet iron plates (inset **1**). It is worn by guardsmen on the Arch of Galerius.

Like the guardsmen on the Arches of Galerius and Constantine, our veteran *eques* is protected by scale armour. The torque worn around the neckguard of his eagle-crested helmet is a new type of military decoration (cf. *AE* 1983, 59; torques are worn by some soldiers on the Arch of Constantine). The veteran's sword is based on an example from Cologne, dating to the late third or early fourth century AD. The insets show details of its ivory hilt (**5**), and front and rear and views of its round silver chape, which is inlaid with niello (**6**). The other swords shown, based on examples from Vimose, are a long thrusting blade (**3**) and a medium-length cut-and-thrust weapon with a pattern-welded blade (**4**).

1

5

4

2

3

6

ABOVE Gravestone of Aurelius Dizala, a Thracian *eques singularis* of the third century AD. Dizala, who died after 20 or more years' service, is immortalized as a triumphant hunter. His groom stands behind, offering up his master's helmet (*CIL* VI 3202). (RHC Archive)

BELOW Funerary portrait of Aurelius Mucianus, a praetorian of *c.* AD 212–238 (*CILVI* 2602). An eagle-hilted sword is suspended from his baldric and he holds a heavy *pilum* with two weights. The bands on the shaft may represent painted or carved decoration, or some form of binding. (© Steven D. P. Richardson)

Equites singulares Augusti

The creation date of the Imperial Horse Guards is uncertain. They were certainly in existence before AD 117 (Speidel 1994b, no. 20), and some became veterans in AD 118 (*RMD* 231). It is tempting to see them as originating from the provincial German horse guard Trajan brought to Rome when he succeeded Nerva in AD 98. Following the mutiny of the praetorians in AD 97 (below), the new emperor certainly needed a trustworthy bodyguard. Domitian is another contender for creator of the *equites singulares* (Speidel 1994a, 35–44). Some early horse guardsmen bear the emperor's family name of Flavius (Speidel 1994b, no. 684), and it has been argued that Hyginus describes the camp of Domitian's field army in the war against the Marcomanni in AD 89.

The campaigns of Trajan and Marcus Aurelius (r. AD 161–180) are also possibilities for the composition of the *de Munitionibus Castrorum*, but, despite the uncertainty over its date, it envisages the presence of up to 900 *equites singulares Augusti* in the camp (8). When the *numerus* (unit) went on campaign, it was usual for a small number of veterans to maintain a skeleton garrison at Rome (cf. Herodian 7.11.12), and so the optimum number of *equites singulares* in the second century AD was probably 1,000. Shortly after his accession in AD 193, Septimius Severus doubled the size of the Horse Guard. A second *numerus* was created and housed in the Castra Nova, the 'New Fortress', next door to the Horse Guards' original camp on the Caelian Hill, which was thereafter known as the Castra Priora, the 'Old Fortress' (Speidel 1994a, 57–60).

The *numeri* of the Horse Guard were commanded by tribunes. They were aided by *exercitatores* (above). Each *numerus* was subdivided into *turmae*, probably of 32 men (implied by Arrian, *Tactica* 18). A *turma* was led by a decurion, and had its own *signifer* (*CIL* VI 3304).

EQUIPMENT AND APPEARANCE

Pilum and lancea

One of the earliest depictions of an Imperial praetorian is on the gravestone of the *speculator* Orfius (*CIL* XI 6125; Franzoni 1987, 118). He holds a regular *pilum*, but monuments of the later first century AD, for example the gravestone of Naevius Verus and the Cancelleria Reliefs of Domitian and his guardsmen, show *pila* with round or ovoid metal weights (*Supplementa Italica* 18 (2000), 362–363; Rankov 1994, 46–47). In the third century AD, praetorians, and even some *equites singulares Augusti*, are depicted on their gravestones holding heavy *pila* with one or two weights (Speidel 1994b, nos 565, 567, 580). Interestingly, on some of these later depictions, the *pila* do not have the usual pyramidal heads; the shanks of the weapons taper to sharp points. The latest praetorian tombstone of this type probably dates to the period AD 293–305. It suggests that the praetorians who fought at the Milvian Bridge still used *pila* (Rocchetti 1967–68).

The *lancea*, usually a light javelin (the word could refer to a range of shafted weapons), was associated with the *speculatores* of the first century AD. According to Suetonius, the emperor Claudius 'never ventured to go to a banquet without being surrounded by *speculatores* with *lanceae*' (*Claudius* 35.1), and during Galba's journey through Italy to Rome in

Aurelius Abitus (left) and Aurelius Vincentius (right), praetorians of the later third century AD (*ILS* 2043, 2038). Abitus has an eagle-hilted sword and his weighted *pilum* tapers to a sharp point. Vincentius' gravestone is unusual in depicting a shield. (© RHC Archive)

AD 68, he was accidentally jabbed by the *lancea* of a *speculator* (*Galba* 18.1). Some of Maxentius' praetorians, infantry and cavalry bore the rank of *lanciarius*, marking them out as specialists with this weapon (*CIL* VI 2787; *ILS* 2791).

Swords and daggers

Funerary and triumphal monuments show that before the third century AD, guardsmen used the same short or medium-length cut-and-thrust swords as other Roman infantry and cavalry, but probably with fancily decorated hilts, scabbards and belts. The daggers of the praetorians dismissed by Septimius Severus were 'inlaid with silver and gold' (Herodian 2.13.10).

Mainz-type *gladii* of the early first century AD. This type of sword is depicted on the gravestone of the praetorian Gaius Firmidius (*CIL* V 912). (© Florian Himmler)

37

LEFT Detail of the eagle-hilted sword and ring-buckle belt of Aurelius Vitalianus, a praetorian of the third century AD (*AE* 1990, 62). (© Florian Himmler)

RIGHT Large daggers of the third century AD. In AD 268, a praetorian or *eques singularis* used such a dagger to save the empress Salonina from kidnappers. (© Florian Himmler)

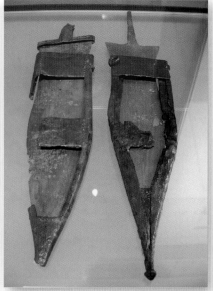

The funerary monuments of praetorians and *equites singulares Augusti* of the third century AD often show medium-length swords with hilts in the form of an eagle's head: the head forms the pommel, and the elongated neck acts as the grip. Similar swords are worn by Diocletian and his co-emperors on the

D SHIELDS AND WEAPONS

Praetorian shields

Left: small *parma* of the type carried by praetorian standard-bearers on Trajan's Column, which commemorates the Dacian Wars of AD 101–102 and 105–106. The pattern on this shield is modelled after the example carried by one of the guardsmen escorting Domitian (r. AD 81–96) on the Cancelleria Relief (Rankov 1994, 46). The same guardsman holds a distinctive lance with a heart-shaped head, which may identify him as a *speculator*. Titius Celer, a *speculator* of the second century AD, is depicted on his gravestone with a similar shield (*AE* 1931, 91).

Centre: hexagonal shield with large scorpion badges, based on the example used by a praetorian cavalryman on the Great Trajanic Frieze (c. AD 117–120). The same monument shows another praetorian trooper with a shield with foliate decoration, but the cheek-piece of his helmet is embossed with a scorpion (Rankov 1994, 53, 55).

Right: curved oval *scutum* modelled on an example carried by another of Domitian's praetorians, on a monument from Puteoli. The scorpion badge, known also from the praetorian standards carved on the funerary monument of Pompeius Asper (*ILS* 2662), was clearly the emblem of the Praetorian Guard in the first and second centuries AD.

Praetorian weapons

Top: decorative lance modelled after the example held by the *parma*-bearer on the Cancelleria Relief. It has been suggested that the eroded weapon depicted on the gravestone of Sulpicius Peregrinus, a *speculator* of the first century AD, was of this type (Speidel 1994a, 33–34). It is possible that the Cancelleria 'lance' is actually a small standard.

Middle: *pilum* with flat-tanged shank and metal weight based on the examples carried by praetorians on the Cancelleria Relief (Rankov 1994, 46).

Bottom: heavy *pilum* with two weights and a socketed shank that tapers to a point, modelled after the examples on the gravestones of Aurelius Lucianus and Aurelius Abitus, praetorians of the third century AD. It is uncertain whether the horizontal bands on the shafts of the weapons were meant to represent painted or carved decoration, or even binding.

Far left: cut-and-thrust sword with eagle-hilt after the example on the gravestone of Aurelius Vitalianus, a praetorian of the mid-third century AD (*AE* 1990, 62), and a contemporary blade of typical form.

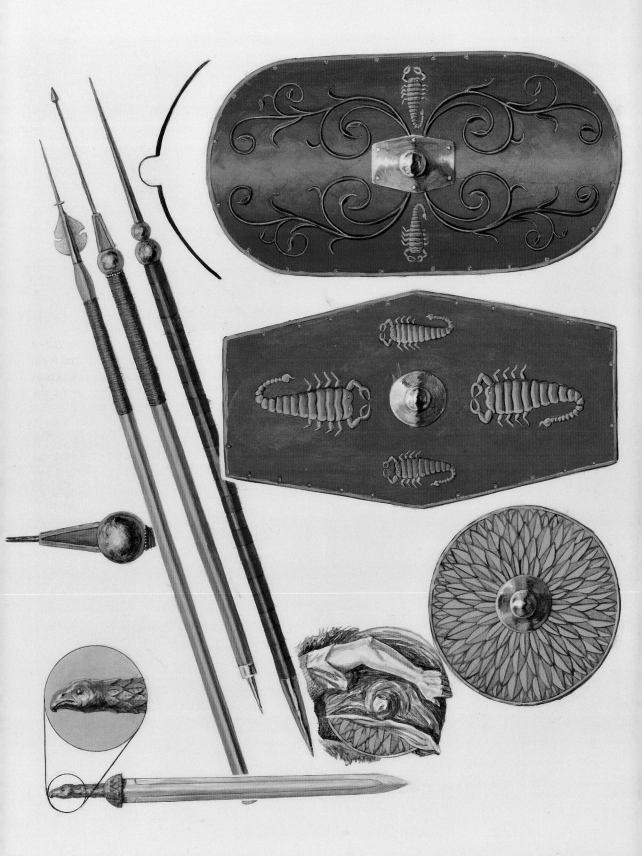

Relief of soldiers, possibly guardsmen, from Galerius' palace at Romuliana. The foot soldier is equipped in the typical fashion of the late third and early fourth centuries AD: ridge helmet, long-sleeved mail shirt and round shield. The cavalryman, wearing a fashionable 'pillbox' hat, is armed with an axe. (© A. Chen/ISAW)

famous porphyry sculpture of the Tetrarchs in Venice. It is uncertain why daggers were not included in the funerary iconography of this period. They were certainly still used by guardsmen. In AD 268, a praetorian or *eques singularis* used his dagger to save the empress Salonina from kidnappers sent by the renegade general Aureolus (Zonaras 12.25).

Other weapons

As we have seen, praetorians and *equites singulares* were trained in archery. The rank of archer (*sagittarius*) did not exist in the guards units of our period, but some men were certainly specialists. Flavius Proclus, an *eques singularis*, is depicted on his gravestone as a horse archer (*AE* 1962, 289), and the grave goods of Marcus Severus, a mounted praetorian *singularis*, included an arrowhead (Abramić & Colnago 1909, 58–59). A relief at Galerius' palace at Romuliana shows a (possible) horse guardsman with a battleaxe.

LEFT Legionary helmet of the first century AD. The more accurate depictions of helmets on a few praetorian gravestones (e.g. Gaius Firmidius), confirm that infantry guardsmen used the same types as the legionaries. (© Florian Himmler)

RIGHT Detail of the much-restored relief on base of the Column of Antoninus Pius (AD 161), depicting praetorians in cuirasses of *lorica segmentata* and holding oval shields. (© R. Rumora/ISAW)

Details of the bronze scales from a shirt of *lorica squamata*. Scale armour was associated with guardsmen in the third and early fourth centuries AD. (© Florian Himmler)

Helmets and armour

No funerary monument of a guardsman depicts him in armour, but some do show helmets, confirming that praetorians used the same iron and bronze types as legionaries (cf. *CIL* V 912; Franzoni 1987, tav. 3). In the third century AD, the gravestones of *equites singulares Augusti* often show the deceased being presented with a helmet crested with an eagle's head.

Triumphal and other state monuments, such as Trajan's Column, the Great Trajanic Frieze, the base of the Column of Antoninus Pius, the Column of Marcus Aurelius and the Aurelian Panels, show praetorians in the full range of Roman armour (*lorica*): hamata (mail), *squamata* (scale) and *segmentata* (articulated plates). In the third century AD, shirts of iron or bronze scales were associated with the praetorians (Dio 78.37.4). The guardsmen wearing long-sleeved shirts of scale and spangenhelms (helmets composed of riveted plates) on the Arch of Galerius, are probably to be identified as praetorians. The battle of the Milvian Bridge relief on the Arch of Constantine shows Maxentius and his cavalry guardsmen drowning in the River Tiber. Like the guardsmen of Galerius, they wear long-sleeved shirts of scale, and must represent Maxentius' mounted praetorians or *equites singulares*.

LEFT The emperor surrounded by his infantry guards (probably praetorians) on the Arch of Galerius, a monument to his triumph over the Persians in AD 298. Note the long-sleeved scale shirts, large round shields and helmets of spangenhelm type. (© G. Churchard)

BELOW Fragment of the funerary monument of a praetorian veteran from Picenum in Italy, who had served as an *eques* and *signifer*. Note the extensive array of decorations for valour (crowns, torques, armlets, harness of *phalerae*), and the crested helmet, long lance, oval shield and full-length greaves. (RHC Archive)

Shields

In the first century AD, praetorian infantry used curved oval *scutum*-type shields. In AD 218, praetorians were still using the *scutum*, perhaps the semi-cylindrical (cf. Dio 78.37.4: 'gutter-shaped shields'), but the gravestone of Aurelius Vincentius, perhaps dating to the later third century AD, shows the deceased praetorian with an oval shield (*ILS* 2038). The guardsmen on the Arch of Galerius carry large, round shields. Standard-bearers and some *speculatores* employed a small, round shield (*parma*). Praetorian cavalry and *equites singulares* were protected by oval and hexagonal shields.

Distinctive clothing

To maintain the fantasy that the emperor was not a military dictator, the praetorians might wear the civilian toga while on duty at the palace or when escorting him in Rome or Italy (Tacitus, *Histories* 1.38; Historia Augusta, *Marcus Antoninus* 27.3).

There was a military boot known as the *caliga speculatoria*, which was favoured by Caligula (the name derives from the little military boots he wore as a child), and is naturally associated with the praetorian *speculatores* (Suetonius, *Caligula* 52). However, the possible *speculator* on the Cancelleria Reliefs wears the same *caligae* (heavy sandals) as his comrades (Rankov 1994, 46).

Insignia

Little is known of the insignia of the *Germani corporis custodes* and *equites singulares Augusti*, but the scorpion was certainly an emblem of the praetorians. It is seen on the praetorians' standards on the monument of Pompeius Asper, and the cheek-guards and shields of praetorian cavalry on the Great Trajanic Frieze. As sole emperor (AD 260–268), Gallienus issued a series of coins celebrating the loyalty of various legions, the *equites singulares* and praetorian cohorts. The legionary coins bear the traditional symbols of those units, but the praetorian coins depict a lion with a radiate crown and not the scorpion; there is no emblem for the *equites singulares*. The lion appears as a shield device on the Arch of Galerius, but more likely to be connected with the praetorians are the shields decorated with the eagle or Hercules. Jupiter (whose symbol was the eagle) and Hercules were the patron deities of the Tetrarchic emperors. It has been assumed that these shields identify soldiers of the recently formed Ioviani and Herculiani legions, but the emblems would also be appropriate to praetorian guardsmen.

Detail of the praetorian on a Domitianic monument from Puteoli. He uses a strap, presumably attached to the handgrip, to carry the curved *scutum* over his shoulder. Note the scorpion badge at the centre of the shield. (© University of Pennsylvania Museum of Archaeology and Anthropology)

E **CAVALRY COMBAT TECHNIQUES**

The praetorian cavalry and *equites singulares Augusti* included men who specialized in the use of the bow and light javelin (*lancea*). Here we see *equites singulares* of the early second century AD practising the famous 'Parthian shot' (bottom), a technique that enabled a horse archer to loose arrows at his enemies even as he galloped away from them, and throwing javelins from horseback (top). Josephus notes that Roman cavalrymen carried *lanceae* in a quiver (*Jewish War* 3.96). Roman cavalry did not use stirrups but the horned saddles, illustrated here, which provided archers and javelineers with a stable fighting platform.

The funerary monument of Pompeius Asper, a career centurion of the later first century AD, who served in the Guard and several legions (*ILS* 2662). The detailed sculptures of the standards of the third praetorian cohort bear the *scorpio* emblem of the Guard, images of the imperial family and crowns recalling battle honours. (© RHC Archive)

DAILY LIFE

The legionaries' view

A legionary of the early Roman Empire could be forgiven for thinking that his counterpart in the Praetorian Guard had it easy. As we have seen, the praetorian received at least twice, if not three times as much pay as the legionary. The praetorian would eventually earn a free grain ration, and the imperial treasury would cover the cost of periods of leave. Gifts of cash from the emperor called *donativa* were more likely to be received by praetorians, and the scale of gifts for praetorians (and presumably other guardsmen) was higher than that given to legionaries.

Above all, the legionary, based on a distant frontier, believed that the praetorian's life was characterized by easy soldiering – if indeed it could be called soldiering – in Rome, guarding the emperor's palace and providing escorts for him and other members of the imperial family. 'The legionaries did not disparage guard duty at Rome, but their own lot was cast among savage peoples, with the enemy visible from their very tents' (Tacitus, *Annals* 1.17).

Tales of the praetorians' 'labours' in and around Rome can hardly have helped to dispel this common view. Was Vinnius Valens, a centurion of the emperor Augustus' praetorian cohorts, famous for pitting his immense strength against the battle lines of the enemy, as a true Roman warrior should? No. 'Valens served as a centurion in the Praetorian Guard of the divine Augustus. He was in the habit of holding carts laden with wine-sacks up in the air until they were emptied, and of catching hold of wagons with one hand and stopping them by throwing his weight against the teams drawing them, and doing other marvellous exploits which can be seen carved on his monument' (Pliny, *Natural History* 7.82). The funerary monument does not survive.

Valens was an apt *name*, meaning 'powerful' or 'vigorous'. When he was not indulging in such trials of strength, Valens acted as a courier, not carrying important military dispatches, but rather volumes of poetry. Horace joked about Valens having to carry his 'weighty' tomes of poetry to Augustus (perhaps in 23 BC): 'Your vigour will help carry the load over hills, rivers and through marshes.' Horace also revelled in the possibility that Valens' fellow-soldiers might learn of the distinctly un-warlike task, of how he had 'sweated carrying these verses,' and mock him mercilessly for it (*Letters* 1.13).

The legionary might go on to wonder, what arduous campaigns did the praetorians of the emperors Caligula and Nero fight in? At least some of the praetorian cohorts of the emperor Tiberius fought in the great battle of Idisiovisa in AD 16 (Tacitus, *Annals* 2.16.3, 20.3), and Claudius' guardsmen had seen action in the invasion of Britain in AD 43 (*ILS* 2648), but Caligula's praetorian cavalry and *Germani* did no more than participate in an apparently farcical reconnaissance across the Rhine against imaginary enemies in AD 39–40 (Suetonius, *Caligula* 45.1). A detachment of Nero's praetorians followed the river Nile south into Ethiopia, carrying out a detailed reconnaissance for a proposed campaign of conquest (Pliny, *Natural History* 6.181), but for other Neronian praetorians going on expedition meant accompanying the emperor on his indulgent tour of Greece in AD 66–68 (Tacitus, *Histories* 1.20). One can only wonder at the contempt the legionaries must have felt at the news that Nero's guardsmen were employed to lead the applause at his theatrical performances in Rome and elsewhere, and faced enemies no more threatening than those unfortunate civilians in the audience who were not enthused by the emperor's artistry. The praetorians encouraged such spectators to demonstrate their appreciation by beating them (Tacitus, *Annals* 14.15; 16.5).

Nero may have been disheartened to learn that the cheerleading of the praetorians was probably not genuine. Some were baffled by his cultural leanings (Suetonius, *Nero* 21.3); others, especially centurions and tribunes were dismayed by it and considered his more outlandish and effeminate antics an affront to their honour (Tacitus, *Annals* 15.67.2, 68.1; Dio 62.24.2). It is not coincidental that the praetorians were persuaded to abandon the emperor soon after returning from Greece (Tacitus, *Histories* 1.5 notes their uneasiness at the betrayal).

The contempt felt by the legionaries towards the praetorians was reciprocated. The predominantly Italian praetorians saw themselves as true Roman soldiers, and dismissed the legionaries, increasingly recruited from the frontier provinces, as barbarians.

When the legionaries of Vitellius attempted to oust the praetorians of Otho from the walls of Placentia, their attacks were verbal as well as physical. The Vitellians shouted insults at the praetorians, calling them 'lazy shirkers, corrupted by the circus and the theatre'. The praetorians yelled back that their enemies were foreigners and savages (Tacitus, *Histories* 2.21, but note 2.66 where Othonian praetorians support legionaries in a dispute with Batavian auxiliaries). A well-known inscription from Aquileia in north-eastern Italy still declares the thoughts of Manlius Valerianus, a retired praetorian centurion: 'I faithfully commanded a century in a praetorian cohort, not in a barbarian legion!' (*ILS* 2671).

Gold coin issued by Claudius depicting the Castra Praetoria. Claudius owed his elevation to the praetorians (AD 41), and on the anniversary of his accession he would reward them with a donative and games. (© Cafuego)

In AD 218, praetorians and legionaries found themselves on opposite sides in the civil war between Macrinus and Elagabalus. In a battle near Antioch, the praetorians, forming the main strength of the army of the emperor Macrinus (recently elevated from the post of praetorian prefect), stripped off their regular heavy scale armour to charge all the more swiftly at their enemies. The guardsmen inflicted a serious mauling on the legionaries who had been bribed to fight for Elagabalus, but Macrinus panicked and fled the battlefield, giving victory to the young pretender (Dio 78.37.4; Herodian 5.4.8). Interestingly, the principal legion in Elagabalus' army was *II Parthica*, based near Rome at Albanum. Inscriptions show that some military families had sons serving in the Guard and *II Parthica* (*CIL* VI 2579, 32690).

The east wall of the Castra Praetoria. The massive fortress still dominates modern Rome. (© RHC Archive)

Service in the Guard

Was life in the Praetorian Guard really much easier than that of the legions? The young praetorian *tiro* (recruit), especially one not yet *immunis* ('immune' from fatigues), may not have thought so. For a 17 year old in a city where epidemics were rife and average life expectancy could be shockingly low, the prospect of at least 16 *stipendia* may well have seemed daunting. Data collected from inscriptions suggests that only 42 per cent survived to complete their service.

Despite his superior status and pay, the praetorian's living conditions in Rome were cramped. Legionary fortresses were designed to accommodate *c*.5,000 soldiers. The Castra Praetoria was only two-thirds the size of the

The north-east corner of the Castra Praetoria. The line approximately halfway up the wall marks the original height of the parapet walkway when the fortress was completed in AD 23. (© RHC Archive)

Funerary relief showing Caelius Arventus, a trooper of the fifth praetorian cohort, and his horse. First century AD (*ILS* 9064). (© RHC Archive)

average legionary base, but by the early third century AD it housed the ten milliary praetorian cohorts and three urban cohorts. It was not until the AD 270s that the urban soldiers were accommodated in their own fortress. Numerous small barrack rooms called *contubernia* were built into the concrete walls of the Castra Praetoria and multi-storey barracks further maximized the available space.

One wonders where stabling was found for the mounts of the praetorian cavalry and the *speculatores*. The number of horses would have been far greater than the number of troopers, because under-officers, who formed the front rank of any formation, required several remounts (Hyginus' *de Munitionibus Castrorum* 7, 16). In auxiliary cavalry forts, the barracks were divided, with rooms on one side for the soldiers and stabling on the

LEFT Praetorian standard on the Arch of the Argentarii with images of the emperors Caracalla (top) and Septimius. There was originally a third portrait, of Caracalla's younger brother, Geta. It was removed in AD 212 following his murder by Caracalla. Below the portraits is a fine depiction of mural crown, perhaps referring to the praetorians' role in the capture of Ctesiphon, the capital of the Parthian Empire, in AD 198. (© RHC Archive)

RIGHT The stick held by the praetorian Aurelius Vitalianus is probably to be identified with the *fustis*, which was used for crowd control and to inflict punishment. (© Florian Himmler)

other. It is uncertain whether praetorians lived so close to their mounts, but strong bonds were certainly fostered. When Septimius Severus disbanded the Praetorian Guard, one distraught praetorian cavalryman refused to give up his beloved horse. The soldier killed the horse and then killed himself (Dio 74.1.2).

The praetorian's high pay (assuming the centurion had not relieved him of most of it) meant he had plenty of cash with which to enjoy himself in the fleshpots of Rome, but he was also likely to relax in the baths at the Castra Praetoria and drink with his comrades (Herodian 4.4.5; Tacitus *Histories* 1.80 for drunkenness in camp).

Guard duty

At the eighth hour (the hour of the day being calculated from dawn) a cohort would leave the Castra Praetoria and march up to the *palace*, remaining there until relieved the following day. The centuries presumably operated a system of rotation. A number of guardsmen were always in close attendance on the emperor and would deal severely with anyone who got too close. In AD 14, the senator Quintus Haterius came to the palace to apologize for a remark that had offended Tiberius. He grovelled at Tiberius' feet, but the emperor, attempting to get past, tripped and fell on his face. Haterius was immediately set upon by guardsmen and almost beaten to death (Tacitus, *Annals* 1.13).

Security was enhanced by the use of a watchword that the tribune commanding the cohort received personally from the emperor. The watchword given by the new emperor Pertinax in January AD 193 was 'Militemus', which means 'Let us be soldiers' (Historia Augusta, *Pertinax* 5.7). The praetorians took offence at it. Still smarting at their failure to protect Commodus from a court plot, the praetorians believed Pertinax was casting aspersions on their abilities as soldiers. Discontent grew and three months later a band of praetorians marched out of the Castra Praetoria in close battle order. They advanced into the *palace* and killed Pertinax and his chamberlains. The praetorian cohort on guard duty, as well as the *equites singulares Augusti* present, stood by and watched the despised emperor die. The soldiers celebrated by restoring the images of beloved Commodus to their standards (Dio 73.9–10; Herodian 2.5.1–6.11).

Riots

The legionary mutineers of AD 14 may have decried the praetorians as mere sentries, but Rome was a violent place and there were outbreaks of civil unrest in Italy. In AD 15, disorder in a theatre at Rome resulted in the deaths of several praetorians and a centurion, while a tribune was wounded (Tacitus, *Annals* 1.77), but some riots were far more catastrophic and the drills practised on the Campus Cohortium proved useful against the urban mob.

In AD 238, the Castra Praetoria was manned only by a small number of *remansores* (the 'remainder', praetorians nearing the end of their service), while the rest of the Guard was abroad campaigning with the emperor Maximinus. The fortress was besieged by a mass of plebs and gladiators loyal to the recently declared emperors Pupienus and Balbinus. We have seen how guardsmen were instructed in archery, and the praetorian veterans used their bows to deadly effect, shooting down their attackers. When the besiegers least expected it, the veterans sallied out. The besiegers were stunned that so few would attack so many. The praetorians killed all of the gladiators and pursued the civilians for a short distance before returning to the fortress. The siege was renewed, but assaults made by the rabble were always beaten back. Eventually, the commanders appointed by Pupienus and Balbinus decided to cut the water pipes running into the fortress. At this point, the praetorians made another sally, routed their opponents and forced them into the narrow streets of Rome. Here matters turned against the praetorians. The civilians rushed into the upper storeys of the tall tenements, some onto the roofs, and began to pelt the soldiers with tiles, masonry and other makeshift missiles. The praetorians presumably formed a *testudo*, the famous 'tortoise' formation of overlapping shields, to protect themselves (the same formation was used to protect Didius Iulianus from the mob), and they used another old tactic; they set fire to the buildings, causing great devastation (Herodian 7.11–12; 2.6.13 for the *testudo*). The praetorians had deliberately set fire to properties in Rome during a major disturbance sometime in the AD 220s: 'the populace, fearing the whole city would be destroyed, came to terms with them' (Dio 80.2.3).

Rioting was hardly a daily occurrence in Rome, but there was a regular need for crowd control at public festivals, the theatres and other spectacles, and especially when the emperor, or members of the imperial family, moved around the city. In AD 18, Tiberius ordered two cohorts to meet Germanicus (the father of Caligula) and escort him into Rome, but all of the praetorians in the city rushed out to greet the charismatic prince (Suetonius, *Caligula* 4). The emperor Claudius (Germanicus' brother) seems to have had far fewer praetorians to protect him in AD 51, when an angry mob surrounded him in the Forum, demanding to know what he intended to do about an acute shortage of food in the city. The praetorians enclosed Claudius, burst through the mob and rushed him back to the Palace (Tacitus, *Annals* 12.43).

A full-sized escort of praetorians would have formed a dense cordon around the emperor while he was on the move, and blocked off streets and the entrances of buildings while he was inside (Tacitus, *Annals* 16.27.1; the escort could include 'plain clothes men' wearing togas). When the crowds surged forward, the praetorians were not gentle and were fully prepared to use their swords (cf. Tacitus, *Annals* 14.61.1).

In AD 312 the Milvian Bridge was located some distance north of Rome. It is now surrounded by the sprawl of the modern city. The battle between Maxentius and Constantine, where the Praetorian Guard made its last stand, was fought to the right of the picture. (© A. Majanlahti)

Maxentius and his scale-armoured cavalry guardsmen drown in the waters of the Tiber. Relief on the Arch of Constantine. (© Florian Himmler)

Relations with the citizenry were not always bad. In contrast to their antics in the AD 220s and 238, when they deliberately set fire to buildings during battles with the plebs, on other occasions the praetorians helped tackle conflagrations (Dio 57.14.10; Suetonius, *Tiberius* 50.3). An inscription from Ostia, the port of Rome, honours a praetorian of the sixth cohort (his name is lost) who died while firefighting. The grateful people of Ostia paid for his funeral (*ILS* 9494).

GUARDSMEN ON THE TRAIL OF BANDITS, EARLY THIRD CENTURY AD

The depredations of *latrones* (bandits) were a chronic problem in Italy and the provinces. Guardsmen were frequently employed in missions against bandits. Here we see a praetorian cavalryman inspecting the tracks left by the band of Bulla Felix, a notorious bandit whose activities enraged the emperor Septimius Severus. He was eventually caught by a detachment of cavalry guardsmen led by a tribune (Dio 76.10; it is uncertain if he was a tribune of the praetorians or the *equites singulares*).

The guardsman is based on the funerary relief of Aurelius Saturninus. Originally a *tesserarius* in *legio II Italica*, he won transfer to the Guard and became a cavalryman of the eighth praetorian cohort (*ILS* 2054). The short-sleeved tunic, close-fitting trousers and open-topped shoes follow the clothing on Saturninus' gravestone, as does the spear with feathers tied beneath the head, which probably identified him as a cavalry scout and messenger (cf. Plutarch, *Otho* 4.2). The sword, scabbard, baldric, and belt decorated with *VTERE FELIX* ('use happily' or 'use with luck') plates, follows an example buried with a casualty of the battle of Lugdunum (AD 197).

Civil unrest

In AD 24, the slave revolt instigated by Titus Curtisius (a praetorian veteran) at Brundisium, was promptly quelled by marines who happened to be in the vicinity, and by a force of praetorians sent from Rome. In AD 64, a detachment of soldiers, probably praetorians, defeated an attempt by gladiators to break out of the imperial gladiatorial barracks at Praeneste (Tacitus, *Annals* 4.27; 15.46). When the urban mob of Pollentia prevented the funeral of a chief centurion and violently extorted cash from his family for a gladiatorial show, the emperor Tiberius dispatched a praetorian cohort to restore order (Suetonius, *Tiberius* 37.3). Nero sent a praetorian cohort to Puteoli, where the plebs had been protesting violently against the greed of local magistrates and gentry (AD 58). A praetorian cohort was dispatched and it so terrorized the population that 'harmony' was quickly restored (Tacitus, *Annals* 13.48).

Bandits (*latrones*) were a major problem and the emperors sent guardsmen or praetorian-led detachments to hunt them down. In AD 246, the *evocatus* Aurelius Munatianus led 20 marines (detached from the Ravenna fleet) in pursuit of bandits in Umbria (*ILS* 509). A tribune of the Guard was responsible for the capture of the infamous bandit Bulla Felix in AD 207 (Dio 76.10). Maternus, another dangerous bandit leader who built up a sizeable force of deserters and criminals, was a former soldier, perhaps a praetorian. In *c.* AD 187, he planned to disguise his men as praetorians and assassinate Commodus at a public festival in Rome. However, the plot was revealed by some of Maternus' discontented underlings, who were less than thrilled at the prospect of his seizing the throne (Herodian 1.10–11).

Belief and belonging

The praetorians failed to protect the emperor Domitian from a deadly court plot in AD 96. But they did not fail to avenge him. Enraged that the ringleaders, the praetorian prefect Petronius Secundus and the chamberlain Parthenius, had not been executed by the new emperor, Nerva, the praetorians mutinied in October AD 97 and held Nerva hostage in the palace. The elderly ruler was so terrified that he vomited and soiled himself. The prefect and chamberlain were delivered up to the vengeful praetorians. Secundus was dispatched with a single blow, but before Parthenius was killed, he was castrated and his severed genitals were stuffed into his mouth. Nerva was then compelled to thank the soldiers publicly for punishing the murderers (Pliny, *Panegyric* 6.1–2; *Epitome de Caesaribus* 12.7–8).

The emperor Maximinus Daia (d. AD 313). The nephew of Galerius, he saw service as a *scutarius* guardsman and *protector*. (© RHC Archive)

The Praetorian Guard is infamous for making and breaking emperors, but assassinations were invariably carried out by small factions within the Guard, and murderers were usually motivated by affronts to their honour: Caligula was killed for insulting a praetorian tribune; Galba because of his failure to deliver a promised donative; Caracalla for failing to deliver an expected promotion; Elagabalus for effeminacy and un-Roman behaviour. More often than not, the praetorians were faithful, especially to generous and charismatic rulers. One example will suffice. Their devotion to Otho, the short-lived emperor of AD 69, was extraordinary, and many *speculatores* and praetorians committed suicide beside his funeral pyre (Tacitus, *Histories* 2.49; Plutarch, *Otho* 17).

BATTLE

The literary evidence for guardsmen in battle is mostly concerned with those enrolled in praetorian cohorts.

The Late Republic

We first encounter a praetorian cohort in action at the battle of Pistoria (62 BC). The cohort appears to have been held in reserve until Marcus Petreius personally led it in a charge against the centre of Catiline's army. The result was decisive; Catiline's line was broken and most of his men were killed (Sallust, *Catiline* 60.5). Several praetorian cohorts were involved in a head-on collision at Forum Gallorum (43 BC), and Octavian's praetorians were wiped out (Cicero, *Letters to his Friends* 10. 30; Appian, *Civil Wars* 3.66–70). Marc Antony's praetorians fought on foot against Parthian cavalry in Media and Armenia in 36 BC. Along with the legionaries, they were far superior to the Parthians in hand-to-hand combat (Plutarch, *Antony* 39.2, 5). Republican praetorians were adaptable. At the sea battle of Actium (31 BC), Octavian's praetorians fought as marines (Orosius, *History Against the Pagans* 6.19.8).

The Empire

Praetorians were almost certainly involved in the great conquests of Augustus' reign, but the first clear instance of Imperial praetorians in combat occurs in AD 16. At the battle of Idisiovisa, the centre of Germanicus' line was formed by two praetorian cohorts. When Armininus' Germans were defeated, some fled and others retreated to a fort. The praetorians, led by Germanicus, stormed the fort (Tacitus, *Annals* 2.16, 20).

Gravestone of Valerius Victorinus, a horse guardsman of a *schola palatina*. He was killed at the battle of Chalcedon in AD 324. (© RHC Archive)

In AD 69, praetorian cohorts formed the centre of the Othonian battle lines at Castores and Cremona. In the first battle, the praetorian cavalry was positioned on the flanks of Otho's army and opened the action. They drove the Vitellians back, but a counter-attack resulted in heavy casualties among the praetorian horse. A charge by the praetorian infantry and Othonian legionaries pushed the Vitellians back again (Tacitus, *Histories* 2.24–26). The first battle of Cremona was fought soon after. Wellesley deduced that the praetorians formed the centre of Otho's line and were pitted against Vitellius' *legio I Italica*. The combat was grim, but the praetorians were eventually pushed back (Wellesley 2000, 81–82). Plutarch states that the praetorians, despite being eager for a fight, actually fled from the battlefield at Cremona without striking a blow (*Otho* 12.6). It is impossible to reconcile this apparent act of cowardice with Tacitus' narrative of the battle and its

Details of an altar set up in honour of Sextus Vibius Gallus, a former praetorian centurion (*CIL* III 13648). It depicts his extensive decorations for bravery: bracelets, medallions, three wall and two rampart crowns, one gold crown, five silver spears, and two banners. Gallus is shown riding down two Dacian warriors, thus dating his feats to the Dacian Wars of Domitian or Trajan in the late first and early second centuries AD. (© P. Lemaire)

aftermath, in which enraged praetorians blame the Othonian defeat on unspecified 'treachery' (perhaps a nervous Othonian commander sounded the recall or made a tactical blunder) and were ready to fight on (*Histories* 2.44). Otho's suicide denied them that opportunity, and Vitellius promptly disbanded their cohorts.

On learning of Vespasian's elevation, the Othonian praetorians regrouped and became the 'backbone' of his army in Italy. At the second battle of Cremona, the praetorians were not organized in their former cohorts, but appear to have fought as a single body under a *vexillum* banner (they were presumably subdivided into centuries). They were initially positioned on the right wing of the Flavian army, but were called upon to restore the centre and tackle the Vitellians' massed artillery (Tacitus, *Histories* 3.21, 23; Dio 65.14.2).

No Vitellian praetorians fought at the second battle of Cremona, but three Vitellian cohorts stormed the Capitol (occupied by Vespasian's brother

G **THE LAST STAND OF VITELLIUS' PRAETORIANS, AD 69**

In December AD 69, the Flavian army captured Rome. The toughest fighting was at the Castra Praetoria, held by three of the 16 Vitellian praetorian cohorts (cf. Tacitus, *Histories* 3.78). The assault on the fortress was led by the men they had displaced, the fanatically loyal praetorians of the dead emperor Otho. 'The Flavians employed every device that had ever been invented for the destruction of the strongest cities – the *testudo*, artillery, earthworks and firebrands – shouting that all the labour and danger they had suffered in all their battles would be crowned by this achievement… On the other side, the Vitellians, unequal though they were in numbers and fortune, by striving to spoil the victory … embraced the last solace left to the conquered. Many, mortally wounded, breathed their last on the towers and battlements. When the gates were broken down, the survivors in a solid mass opposed the victors and to a man fell giving blow for blow, dying with their faces to the foe, so anxious were they, even at the moment of death, to secure a glorious end' (Tacitus, *Histories* 3.84).

In the reconstruction, the former Othonians about to lead the final assault through the broken gates are equipped as regular legionaries; when disbanded by Vitellius, they had to hand in their arms and equipment (ibid. 2.67). The legend on their shields declares support for 'Emperor Vespasian!' The band of Vitellian praetorians, seen in a courtyard behind the gates, are equipped with distinctive oval *scuta*-shields, based on those carried by the (probable) praetorians on a relief from the Arch of Claudius (AD 51; Rankov 1994, 20).

Cavalry-sports helmet of the early second century AD, said to have been found in a tomb at Nola and now in the British Museum. The Italian find suggests its owner was a praetorian trooper or an *eques singularis*. (© RHC Archive)

Sabinus, and the urban cohorts). In December AD 69, the ex-Othonian praetorians led the assault on the Castra Praetoria; rather than surrender, the Vitellian praetorians preferred to die and made a famous last stand (Tacitus, *Histories* 3.69–73, 78, 84).

Epigraphic and iconographic evidence, namely inscriptions recording participation in campaigns and awards made for valour, and depictions of guardsmen on victory monuments, provides ample evidence that they fought in the wars of Domitian, Trajan, Lucius Verus and Marcus Aurelius. A spell of inaction during the reign of Commodus (AD 180–192), reinforced the old view of the praetorians as being soft (Dio 73.16.1–3), but Septimius Severus' new guardsmen, selected from the best legionaries, almost met with disaster at Lugdunum in AD 197. Only the intervention of the massed Severan cavalry, which had performed a great outflanking manoeuvre and slammed into the rear of Clodius Albinus' British legions, saved them (Dio 75.6.6–8).

In AD 16, only two cohorts were away from Rome on campaign, but in the Severan era, and presumably throughout the century, all ten praetorian cohorts went to war together (less a few *remansores*, cf. Dio 79.2.3 and Herodian 7.11.2). The epitaph of one Severan praetorian boasts that 'he was in all of the expeditions' (*CIL* VI 2553). With a fighting strength equivalent to two legions, the praetorians formed the core of Macrinus' army in the battle against Elagabalus (fought at a village in the vicinity of Antioch in AD 218). 'So far as the zeal of the praetorians went, he conquered. He had taken away their scale body armour and gutter-shaped shields and had thus rendered them lighter for battle' (Dio 78.37.4). Fighting then, as light infantry, the praetorians inflicted a mauling on Elagabalus' legionaries but, on becoming aware of Macrinus' disgraceful flight from the battlefield, they accepted Elagabalus' offer to become his bodyguard (Herodian 5.4.8–10).

Praetorians and *equites singulares* would have followed Maximinus (a former guardsman) when he became the first Roman emperor to charge into hand-to-hand combat, in a battle against the Alamanni in AD 235 (Herodian 7.2.6–8). Three years later, on the revolt of the Senate and its creation of the emperors Pupienus and Balbinus, Maximinus abandoned operations on the Danube frontier and invaded Italy. He approached Emona, the most north-easterly city of Italy in a defensive formation:

As Maximinus stood on the frontier he sent scouts on ahead to reconnoitre and see whether there were any hidden ambushes laid in the deep mountain

valleys or dense woods. He himself led his army down to the plain and arranged the legionary infantry in a shallow, rectangular formation rather than in depth, so as to extend right across the plain. All the equipment, including the pack animals and carts, were allocated the centre, while he brought up the rear himself with the Guards. On the wings rode the cataphracts [fully armoured heavy cavalry], the Mauretanians, eastern archers, and a large force of allied German cavalry. (Herodian 8.1.1–3)

Scene on the Aurelian Column depicting the emperor Marcus Aurelius (r. AD 161–180) and his mounted bodyguards, the *equites singulares Augusti*, in the field during the Marcomannic Wars. (© RHC Archive)

Trajan's praetorian cavalry and *cornicines* (horn players) in action in a scene from the Great Trajanic Frieze incorporated into the Arch of Constantine. The cavalrymen have scorpion badges on the cheek-pieces of their helmets, while the *cornicines* are identified as praetorians by their distinctive lion skins and scale shirts. (© R. Hall)

Maximinus' army, accustomed to victory in open battle, became bogged down in a siege at Aquileia, and the emperor was murdered by members of *legio II Parthica* and the Praetorian Guard. As usual, his assassination was probably carried out by a small faction; the majority of soldiers were angry and dismayed at the murder of the emperor they had created (Herodian 8.5.8–6.1).

The praetorian cohorts may have faltered against the walls of Aquileia but, as we have seen, at the same time their veteran comrades in Rome defended the Castra Praetoria with great skill and tenacity.

The complex military history of the mid- and late third century AD is obscured by a dearth of sources, in particular good literary sources, but we do know that the praetorians fought with Aurelian against the Palmyres at Emesa in AD 272. According to Zosimus, who drew on a now lost third-century source, the praetorians 'were the most distinguished' of Aurelian's soldiers (1.52).

H **MAXENTIUS' PRAETORIANS AT THE BATTLE OF THE MILVIAN BRIDGE, AD 312**
Here we see Maxentius' praetorians receive the charge of Constantine's cavalry at the battle of the Milvian Bridge. The praetorians wear contemporary iron ridge helmets and are equipped with large round shields, long-sleeved scale or mail shirts following the guardsmen depicted on the Arch of Galerius (a triumphal monument commemorating that emperor's victory over the Persians in AD 298). Galerius' guardsmen carry long thrusting spears, but in this reconstruction Maxentius' praetorians are about to throw *pila* of the type known from the gravestones of praetorians, and some *equites singulares Augusti*, of the third century AD. On one such gravestone, the face of the guardsman appears to be modelled after the official portraiture of the Tertrarchic emperors of AD 293–305 (Rocchetti 1967–68). This suggests that the praetorians still used the heavy weighted *pilum* at the time of the Milvian Bridge.

The final appearance of the praetorian cohorts, and perhaps also the *equites singulares Augusti*, in battle was at the Milvian Bridge in AD 312.

AFTER THE BATTLE

Early on 28 October AD 312 (the sixth anniversary of the day on which the Praetorian Guard had elevated him), the last emperor to rule from Rome consulted the sacred Sibylline Books and discovered an oracle to the effect that an enemy of Rome would die that day. Maxentius was doubtless aware of the ambiguity of the oracle, but he chose to fight. This emperor was no coward and he had a strong army of veteran troops. He led his praetorians, cavalry guard, legionaries (Adams & Brennan 1990) and levies from Italy and North Africa across the bridge of boats to the plain above the Milvian crossing of the Tiber. He then formed a simple battle line – infantry at the centre and cavalry on the flanks–to block Constantine's line of advance down the Flaminian Way. The river was at his soldiers' backs. There was no easy line of retreat.

The battle of the Milvian Bridge was hard fought, but Maxentius' choice of battleground was his undoing. His cavalry and then infantry were gradually forced towards the river; the prospect of death by drowning caused panic and Maxentius' troops broke and fled for the bridge of boats. Only the Praetorian Guard stood firm, covering the retreat of the emperor it had made, but it was for nothing. Constantine pressed his attack and broke through the thinned ranks of the praetorians. Maxentius and his cavalry guard attempted to cross the bridge of boats, but it was already overloaded with fugitives and collapsed. Maxentius and his guardsmen drowned (*Latin Panegyric* 12(9).17; Zosimus 2.16; Speidel 1994a, 152–157 argues that the cavalry guardsmen were *equites singulares*).

The surviving praetorians, trapped on the far bank of the Tiber, were not massacred. Constantine was impressed by their courage. The Praetorian Guard was disbanded for the final time and its barracks were destroyed (Aurelius Victor 40.25; Zosimus 2.17), but the guardsmen were not dishonourably discharged. They were sent north and scattered among the garrisons of the forts on the Rhine and Danube frontiers of Constantine's domains. In AD 313, their successes in combating brigands and raiders were lauded (*Latin Panegryic* 12(9).21.2–3).

Maxentius' Praetorian Guard was created from the rump left at Rome. Diocletian appears to have divided the bulk of the manpower of the cohorts (and perhaps also of the *equites singulares*) between him and the three other

The gravestone of Lucius Avaenius Paser, a praetorian of the first century AD, who served for 14 years in the first cohort (*AE* 1927, 108). He must have seen action for, as well as his helmet, *gladius* and *pugio*, two decorations for valour are depicted, either *armillae* (bracelets) or torques (neck bands). (© Combusken)

Tetrarchs, leaving token elements of all ten cohorts at Rome (Aurelius Victor 39.47). The guardsmen attached to Diocletian's court at Nicomedia were still called praetorians (Lactantius, *de Mortibus Persecutorum* 12.5), but Galerius and Constantius I gave their guardsmen new titles (ibid. 19.6 for Galerius' *scutarii*, 'shield-bearers'; Zosimus 2.9 distinguishes Constantius' 'court soldiers' from the praetorians in Rome). Maxentius' cohorts were filled out by deserters from the legions of Galerius and his co-emperor, Severus (Adams & Brennan 1990).

In AD 324, Constantine defeated Licinius at Chalcedon and reunified the Empire. A horse guardsman called Valerius Victorinus was killed in the battle. He had served for seven years in the 'sacred palace'. It is uncertain whether Victorinus served in the palace of Constantine or Licinius, but he was almost certainly a member of one of the *schola palatina* guards units, now the most senior and prestigious in the Roman Army (*AE* 1976, 631; Speidel 1995). The origins of the *scholae* are uncertain, but the praetorian cohorts bore the title *palatina* in the later third century AD (*RIB* 966; *AE* 1934, 157), and it is tempting to trace the *scholae* back to the detachments of praetorians and *equites singulares* sent to the courts of the Tetrarchs in AD 293.

FURTHER READING

Websites
Most of the inscriptions referred to above (*AE, CIL, ILS, RIB, RMD*), and links to photographs of many, can be found on the Epigraphik-Datenbank Clauss/Slaby:
http://oracle-vm.ku-eichstaett.de:8888/epigr/epigraphik_en
Roman Army Talk is the best forum for discussion of the legions and all other Ancient military matters:
http://www.romanarmytalk.com

References
Abramić, M. & Colnago, A., 'Untersuchungen in Norddalmatien', *Jahreshefte des Österreichischen Archäologischen Institutes in Wien* 12 (1909), Beiblatt 13–112
Adams, J. N. & Brennan, P. M., 'The Text at Lactantius, *De Mortibus Persecutorum* 44.2, and Some Epigraphic Evidence for Italian Recruits', *Zeitschrift für Papyrologie und Epigrafik* 84 (1990), 183–186
Cowan, R., *Roman Legionary, 58* BC–AD *69*, Oxford: 2003
Crawford, M. H., *Roman Republican Coinage*, Cambridge: 1974
Franzoni, C., *Habitus atque Habitudo Militis*, Rome: 1987
Keppie, L., *Legions and Veterans*, Stuttgart: 2000
Passerini, L., *Le Coorti Pretorie*, Rome: 1939
Rankov, B., *The Praetorian Guard*, London: 1994
Rocchetti, L., 'Su una stele del periodo tetrarchico', *Annali della Scuola Archeologica Italiana di Atene*, 45–46 (1967–68), 487–498
Speidel, M. P., *Riding for Caesar*, Cambridge, Mass: 1994a
Speidel, M. P., *Die Denkmäler der Kaiserreiter. Equites singulares Augusti*, Cologne: 1994b
Speidel, M. P., 'A Horse Guardsman in the War Between Licinius and Constantine', *Chiron* 25 (1995), 83–87
Wellesley, K., *The Year of the Four Emperors*, 3rd ed, London: 2000

GLOSSARY

ala	auxiliary cavalry unit
allecti	chosen men
Apollinaris	'of (the god) Apollo', legion title
armatura	advanced weapons drill, also title of instructor of the drill
caetrati	Spanish bodyguards equipped with the small and round *caetra* shield
campidoctor	field instructor
centuria	century, sub-unit of a cohort comprising 80 or 160 soldiers
centurion (*centurio*)	commander of a century
cohors praetoria	in Republican period, either the staff of a general/governor or his bodyguard. In the Empire, a bodyguard unit
cohort (*cohors*)	infantry formation of six centuries
corporis custodes	bodyguard
decuria	cavalry sub-unit of ten or more troopers
decurion (*decurio*)	commander of *decuria* or *turma*
doctor	instructor
eques	cavalryman
Equestrian Order	Rome's upper-middle class
equites singulares Augusti	horse guardsmen of the Augustus, i.e. the emperor
evocatus	veteran recalled to service at the request of his commander or emperor to perform a specialist function
exercitator	senior centurion concerned with training cavalry
Ferrata	'Ironclad', legion title
Gallica	'Gallic' or 'of Gaul', legion title
Gemina	'Twin', legion title
gladius	general term for a sword
immunis	soldier given immunity from performing fatigues
Italica	'Italian', legion title
lancea (or *lancia*)	usually referring to a light javelin, but also a type of dual-purpose throwing and thrusting spear
lanciarius	soldier equipped with the *lancea*
legio	legion
lorica	armour
miles	soldier, infantryman
optio	centurion's deputy, one per century
parma	small round shield carried by standard-bearers and musicians
Parthica	'Parthian', legion title
Pia	'Loyal', honorific title of praetorian cohorts
pilum	javelin with long iron shank
Primigenia	'First-born', legion title
primus pilus	'first spear or *pilum*', leading centurion of the first cohort and most senior in the legion; all praetorian tribunes had served in this rank

protector	in the early third century AD, probably analogous with *singularis*, a bodyguard of junior rank; from the later third century, title of veteran soldiers earmarked for promotion to high rank, perhaps similar to *evocati*
pugio	dagger
sagittarius	archer
scutarius	*scutum*-bearer, title of guardsmen in late third and fourth centuries AD
scutum	oval or semi-cylindrical body shield
Senatorial Order	in Republican times, the ruling class of Rome; remains the upper class in the Empire
sesquiplicarius	soldier receiving pay and a half
signifer	standard-bearer, one per century or *turma*
singularis	guardsman, bodyguard
speculator	scout; soldier of elite corps of Praetorian Guard
stipendium	salary, year of paid service
tector	lit. meaning is 'plasterer', but probably military slang for *protector*, a bodyguard
tesserarius	officer of the watchword, one per century
tiro	recruit
tribune (*tribunus*)	officer of equestrian rank. Commander of a praetorian cohort or the *equites singulares*
turma	cavalry sub-unit of 32 troopers
Vindex	'Avenging', honorific title of praetorian cohorts
vitis	the vine-wood stick of the centurion (and evocatus), insignia of his rank

INDEX